Faith
TO PRODUCE MIRACLES

By

BRENT C. SATTERFIELD, PH.D.

Edited by Jennifer R. Satterfield

BALBOA.
PRESS
A DIVISION OF HAY HOUSE

Balboa Press books may be ordered through booksellers or by contacting:

Balboa Press
A Division of Hay House
1663 Liberty Drive
Bloomington, IN 47403
www.balboapress.com
1 (877) 407-4847

Scripture taken from the King James Version of the Bible

Print information available on the last page.

ISBN: 978-1-5043-9852-7 (sc)
ISBN: 978-1-5043-9854-1 (hc)
ISBN: 978-1-5043-9853-4 (e)

Library of Congress Control Number: 2018902223

Balboa Press rev. date: 02/28/2018

Contents

Preface
Two Levels of Faith

I am a bioengineer by trade. I wanted to understand the physics of disease so that I could help the world's poor. This was an outgrowth of a series of experiences I had in Brazil while living and working among some of the destitute people there. I had been converted to a faith in Christ and decided to spend two years living and working among those who needed help the most. I loved that time so much I decided to find a career that would let me keep working with the world's impoverished.

Over the years, I developed a series of technologies to lower the cost of healthcare in the developing world. But I saw this was not enough. People were still poor in spirit, poor of heart, even if you could provide them with free health care. Further, even if you lowered the cost of healthcare a hundredfold, there were still people in the world who could not afford it, entire countries even who could not access it.

This dilemma I faced with technological innovation continued until a few years ago. At that time I was led by the light of God's voice within me on a journey of deep prayer, meditation, and learning. I was specifically directed to a number of individuals who had learned how to use faith to heal in seemingly impossible ways. My mind was exposed to the possibility that rather than solely innovating in the physical sciences to promote healing, I could study faith the same way I had science. I could set out to comprehend it and then document it in such a way that other people could access it as well. If the principles that allowed the few to understand the faith that works miracles could be adequately described, then those principles could be taught to the masses. The world could change through faith in a way that it could never do through the best innovations in science and capitalism.

I took a break from my career and was led to investigate how faith is used in a variety of religious traditions and cultures in relation to the occurrence of miracles. As a result, I have seen faith in a whole new light, from a perspective which is without religious boundaries. It is this journey of faith and its fruits that I wish to share. I believe it is applicable to people of all religious backgrounds. A deeper understanding and application of faith can enrich the lives of any sincere seeker of God and his light. It is my desire that those who read this book find an increased understanding of how to make their faith work for them in more powerful and miraculous ways.

Among those who attempt to work miracles, I have seen that there are two levels of faith, one of action and one of power. Most of those who adhere to different religions reach the level of faith that is of action. Few, whether through grace or through understanding, ever reach the level of consistent faith that acts as a principle of power. It is the level of faith as a principle of power where miracles come into being. And it is this level of faith where men and women have the power to converse with God and angels.

The first type of faith is a shadow or a type of the second. It is intended to teach how to have faith through physical, mental and emotional action. It includes things like going to Church, confessing Christ, reading scriptures, living a good life, keeping good thoughts in our minds or good feelings in our hearts. In each case, actions are a form of trying to *control* the physical, emotional, mental or spiritual environment. The actions themselves are not the reason that this is a preparatory level of faith, rather it is the subconscious motives as to *why* the actions are done that dictates the expression of faith that is present.

Purify the conscious *and* the subconscious to make the eye of the *entire* mind single to the glory of God.

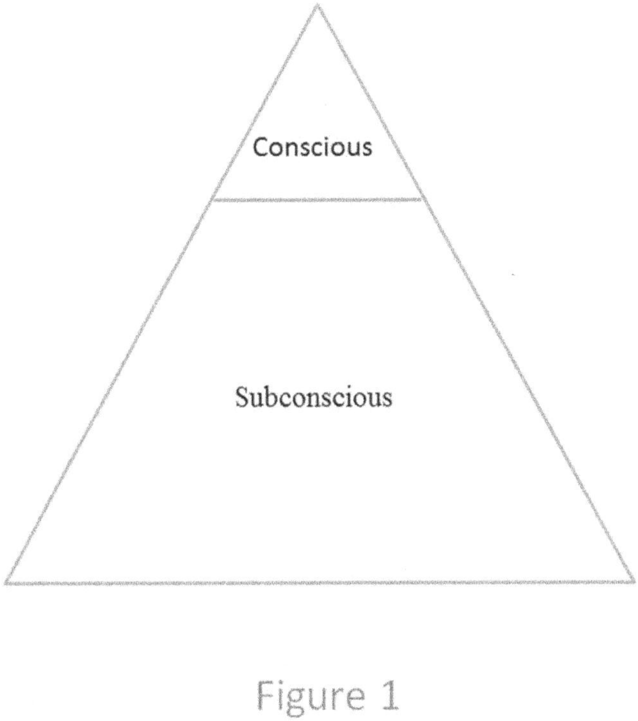

Figure 1

Few people ever pay attention to the subconscious mind. It is easy for us to embrace the recent scientific advances that we see in our lives on a day to day basis. However, we often ignore psychological understandings that have been present for more than two hundred years. Psychologists tell us that the conscious mind is just the tip of the iceberg. To understand what shows up in our conscious experience, we must understand the vast network of subconscious programming that creates our experience. It is this unmapped subconscious network that is the heart that must be purified. It is the lack of purification and sanctification in our hearts that prevents the signs of faith from appearing in our lives that we so diligently seek.

So, faith as a principle of action is not only about the specific things a person *does*, it is *why* they do those things. It is the effort to *control*. For the average person, there is a heavy network of fear, guilt, and shame in the subconscious that a person is trying to avoid. They may use things like spiritual desire or spiritual pride in order to create increased incentive to move into a state of action, where there is a belief that it is by their efforts that conditions will change. For example, a person may pray harder, fast longer, or make other sacrifices to try and bribe God to answer their plea.

Faith as a principle of power recognizes that all real progress comes from God. This type of faith comes from *letting go*. Letting go is essentially the opposite of control. In this type of faith, there is a release of the need to be the doer or to control the outcome. For example, there is a sincere belief that regardless of the outcome, the result will be one of perfect love from God. There is no more spiritual pride that comes into play from accomplishment at this level. In other words, the person "performing" the miracle does not derive any personal value from the experience. They are simply witnesses to God doing a work.

Faith as a principle of action actually dovetails with faith as a principle of power. It is precisely when an individual has satisfied the subconscious law present within them through their actions that they finally let go and allow God to take over and thereby access power. This is why actions appear to have power. When a person who has satisfied their internal need to fast for a certain length of time finally reaches that threshold, they let go and allow God to bless them. Thus, faith as a principle of action serves as the training wheels to focus our intention and access the power within. It is the excuse the conscious mind uses to let go and give God the power to bless us beyond what we have earned.

When an individual uses their agency to release the need to be the one who does the work, then God takes over. It turns out that God loves us so much that if we insist that he cannot help us (eg by saying we need to pray more, repent more, or do any other thing before he can help us), then he won't. But who would ever turn God's help down? The problem is, none of us would consciously. And few of us are aware enough of the subconscious mind to know what is blocking our experience with a more powerful version of faith.

This is the primary aim of this book, to delve into the subconscious motives for our actions and the ways in which we deny God's power in our hearts, even when our minds openly and devotedly seek him. Not only do we explore the emotions that are subconsciously directing our conscious actions, but also look at how to purify and release them. It is ultimately through the purification of our hearts that we obtain the kind of faith that has power, and that we avoid the words of Isaiah, that with their lips they do honor Him, but their hearts are far from Him.

It is not only in the power of faith that the subconscious affects us. During the years, I have seen a number of individuals who have become disillusioned with their religion. They reach a point where their faith no longer works for them. Instead of blessings, they feel that God has failed them. They feel they have been led astray, and their religious world crumbles.

The problem is that many who start on the path to learning faith through action come to believe that the power is in the actions and symbols themselves. This can lead to the eventual fruit of religious action without power. This was the case of the people in Isaiah's day who kept all the law of Moses, it's Sabbaths and temple ordinances and yet were told that their actions were as sin before God. When all the faith that brings power is gone out of an action, it ceases to bless an individual and leaves them trapped behind the onerous weight of having to earn the blessings from God that were once freely offered.

I have since wondered if the appearance of disillusionment is not necessarily due to sin, and is not necessarily a sign that it is time to change religions. Instead, what if disillusionment was merely an invitation to shed the skin of a more superficial relationship with our faith and step into something more whole, more comprehensive? What if it were simply an invitation of the Divine to wake up to greater joy, purpose, and meaning?

Inside of each religion is a nugget of truth, waiting for the sincere seeker to find. Inside of each faith, there is an understanding that needs to be dusted off and extracted from the cultural bounds it is found in. All truth is of great value. Our ability to see past the box to the meat underneath is a big part of our purpose here. In Christian language, it may form the dividing line between the wheat and the tares.

While it may be difficult for us to imagine each religion holding truth, each does, no matter how small. God causes his sun to shine on both the wicked and the righteous. He puts truth in all teachings, however small and insignificant it may appear to us. And all truth is of value.

In science, we understand that physical light is not just comprised of one frequency. We may only see and value the visible spectrum of light in our lives, but that does not mean that ultraviolet or infrared frequencies have no value. In fact, it is only through combining the information gleaned from each of these spectrums that astronomers have put together such revealing views and understandings of the heavens above. It is the same with spiritual light. We may see and judge the world through one filter or frequency, but it is in incorporating all the light that we see clearly that which is above.

For the Christian seeker, it would do us well to remember that the New Jerusalem has twelve gates in it. Like different frequencies of light, there is one for each of the twelve tribes of Israel. Each gate is a reminder to us that the scattered children of God, wherever they have gone, each belong in that Holy City. It is a reminder that the truths they have been sent to find and gather in over the long years are all important for the construction of the heavenly place. If not so, then why not have just one gate or several gates that any tribe can enter in? Why the need for the reminder that each tribe is a custodian of unique truths and understandings?

For those still in the midst of those various religious understandings, we often see outsiders as being misguided, and from the perspective of the frequency of light that we value, they probably are. But consider that the frequencies of light valued by each of these outsiders will be cleaned up and in their time brought into the Holy City in the form of the truths we have yet to see, consider or embrace. They will have the truths that are as important to us as our truths are to them.

The keystone is more than just a big rock when it is holding the other truths together. The crowning jewel is more than just a gem when it is affixed to the crown and is able to bring glory to the whole. All light when it has been purified from the darkness goes into making that full spectrum image of heaven. Regardless which frequency is the capstone and which is the foundation, all are necessary to form the complete understanding of what God seeks to reveal.

Even those who never make it into the Holy City, those who are cast out, even these are necessary for us to find our own way. Without the opposition, there would be no salvation. Without darkness, there would be nothing to be saved from. The entire plan of salvation rests upon the idea that there is *both* light and dark. Thus we see that there is light even in the existence of the darkness. Its appearance is no accident, no misstep by God, no failure on his part due to a lack of power or authority.

All things that are exist and work together for our eternal good. God is really that great.

As we go through our own journey towards that holy place, we can sometimes hit roadblocks. To one who has never had a crisis of faith, maybe this seems unreasonable. We should probably just grit our teeth and have more faith until we get through it. Perhaps there is some truth to this. But to the person who is experiencing the trial of faith, this response lacks compassion and understanding. To the person who is experiencing this very real crisis in their lives, they are struggling with the substance of life and death, with the comprehension of the eternities. There is no greater ordeal through which to pass.

But what if this struggle is not a sign of weakness, rather an invitation from God to grow into a greater light? For the average Christian there are several progressive understandings of faith: 1) Christ's grace is all I need. 2) If I work hard and obey the commandments, God will bless me, and I can control the outcomes in my life. 3) If I learn to control my thoughts and emotions and thereby the creations of my heart, God will bless me and I can control the outcomes in my life. 4) I yield my heart and spirit completely unto God; I give over all control unto him in good times as well as in bad. Perhaps there are more understandings of faith than this. But these summarize some of the basics.

Many converts to Christianity start with a very simple belief about grace. Christ has paid for their sins. That is it. That is the end of the story. But as time goes on, they find that their lives are still difficult. They still have pain. Their reasons for turning to Christ, to solve the pain and problems in their lives, are not being answered. This leads them to a potential first crisis of faith.

In exploring answers to this problem, they may run across the idea that Christ taught them that if they loved him, that they should keep his commandments. They may start trying to bargain with God at a subconscious level, trying to earn his love by doing what they think he wants them to. If grace alone was not enough to buy my way out of suffering and difficulty, then I will try to obligate God to bless me by keeping the law those blessings are based upon.

Once again, a person may follow this level of faith for quite some time. But the day eventually returns when even external obedience is not enough. They are still suffering. Their lives are still full of problems that should not be there if God is blessing them. So they move through the next layer of faith to a more intimate connection with God.

This next layer is characterized by a desire to purify the heart and the mind. Maybe if the heart is right and all the thoughts and emotions therein, then God will bless me. That must be the reason that God is not paying attention to my prayers. For surely, if there were a God, he would not lead me into suffering or trial or difficulty. Surely, he would spare me from these things. Therefore, it must be my fault. I must be doing something wrong.

So again, the Christian seeker moves to purify the heart and mind. Perhaps they have also heard some of the new age philosophies that what we think about comes into being. By controlling our thoughts, perhaps we will finally be free from the negative creations in our lives. But after a time of trying to control all the negative emotions and thoughts, we find that we are still not able to control our lives. We are still not able to bind God. We still run into situations that God could not possibly put us into. So where can we possibly go from this point? There seems to be nothing more we can do to earn his love, to buy his blessings, or to control the circumstances in our lives.

This final crisis of faith is perhaps the most important for the Christian seeker. Out of all the rebirths that we might go through, this is one of the most important, because it leads us back to grace. It leads us back to a fundamental concept of our faith that we overlooked in the beginning: Faith is not about controlling our lives. It is not about controlling our physical, mental, emotional or even spiritual environments. It is not about removing all of the difficulty from our lives. Rather, it is about submission. It is about yielding. It is about letting go. It is about complete and total surrender to God in both the good times as well as the bad. This is where real change begins to happen in the heart of the seeker. This is the revolution of the soul.

In any one of these crises of faith, the believer may choose to change their religious approach. They may choose to walk away from their faith or even from Christ. While changes in religion are sometimes a good thing, that is an extremely personal decision between an individual and God. But for most, a simple acknowledgment that God is calling you to a deeper understanding of the basic meaning of faith and your relationship with Christ is sufficient. Answering that call, rather than running from it, can lead to a much more rewarding comprehension of God. For some, it can lead to the veil being parted and miracles being witnessed.

As before, this progression of understandings of faith in the Christian journey can be simplified into two main levels: faith as a principle of action and faith as a principle of power. During this journey, the Christian started with a seed of faith as a principle of power, but not having a full understanding, soon moved into faith as a principle of action. Even the effort to control thoughts and emotions was an action based type of faith. It was not until the Christian moves back into a state of submission that the heart opens and they begin to experience the fruit of faith as a principle of power again.

It is not that there is no power for the Christian who is in a state of action, just that there are conditions placed upon it. In other words, the Christian's subconscious mind insists that he or she must be more righteous before the miracle occurs. They unconsciously use their agency to tell God when they will or will not accept the miracle. There is an insistence that the action, whatever it may be, be performed to some level of satisfaction before the miracle is granted. Then, there is a submission or allowance by the individual for the miracle to come forth. Thus, even in our actions, it is still by grace that miracles are obtained.

Those who have experienced faith as a principle of power will generally have more satisfaction with their religious or spiritual devotion. It is in the state of true submission where their hearts are changed that they will find more meaning and joy in it. It is ironic that those persons newest to their faith are often the ones that experience this level of depth and see the most miracles, especially because this is exactly opposite of every profession in the world, where those who have been working the longest tend to be the best at what they do. This is because those new to their faith start by letting go. It is only once they think they know that they start trying to do instead of allowing God's perfect grace. It is the complete submission of the new convert or the long-standing disciple that opens the windows of heaven, a perfect trust that whatever is, is right.

In the rest of the book, I will dive into the subconscious factors that are hidden from us as we pursue our faith in whatever religious or philosophical perspective that may be. It is the presence of these subconscious factors that often dictates the level of joy we find in our faith and our ability to see miracles in our lives on a more regular basis.

I have studied and practiced the techniques presented herein on a full-time basis over a period of years. I have seen miraculous changes in myself and others. I have seen people healed of deep emotional and psychological trauma; I have seen physical disease that was medically incurable resolve. Both I and others have had experiences with God that we never thought were possible to have in this life.

I am not the doer any more than anyone else is who has seen miracles. I am not presently in control of the result, and I do not know if I ever will be. I am just a witness in an ever-expanding journey of understanding. It is my joy to watch those who are truly gifted and to learn what I am able. I am still a student of God and miracles and expect that no matter how beautiful the experiences become, I will still be a student. I am always learning.

The ideas presented herein should not be viewed as final understandings. In science, we understand that the best ideas are not fact. They are simply the best understandings we have today. The utility of the model is not based on its correct description of reality so much as its ability to repeatedly predict and produce the desired results. As we learn more, the model will be revised again and again, leading to greater understanding and more powerful results. Whatever understanding we have today is the viewpoint we will wake up from tomorrow as we come into greater and greater perceptions of truth and light. This is the joy of the journey of the true disciple of God.

Even if we were to arrive at a truly accurate model, words are limited. Those who rely on words alone to communicate or to receive information are limited by them. I have seen repeatedly in the spiritual community that those with the greatest knowledge are incapable of finding the words to teach their understanding. The truths held by these men and women are of spirit and need spirit to be understood.

All too often I have heard the communication behind their words saying that the words are a starting point. But to those who cannot hear the message behind the words, they become a trap beyond which the student cannot progress. Many times I have heard the message behind the words telling me something that is almost completely opposite of the surface message. I have heard it telling me the next steps in my personal journey. The words spoken consciously are spoken to the person listening who cannot hear spirit. The fuller message is always evolving and flowing with the individual receiving based on their readiness to hear. The message behind the words changes over time because we change over time. The message behind the words reveals the next step in our personal journey. This is the message I would encourage you to pay attention to in this book, the one that is personalized, behind the words.

If there is anything in this book that offends you, you might take the time to ask the question, "Why?" Offense is most often caused by resonance with unresolved fears or hurts inside of us. When we know the truth and are secure in it, then even incorrect ideas presented by others, whether intentional or not, are no longer offensive. Love is not a defensive energy.

Any offense we experience is an indication of some area in our subconscious that is not fully resolved yet. Pay attention to it. This is the difference between those who have a superficial level of faith and those who go deep enough to heal the trauma that separates them from God. It is in the process of this level of healing that we obtain the faith to work miracles, that we obtain an understanding of the heavens. This does not mean you will agree with everything I say in this book after you complete your healing, but it does mean that you will no longer throw out the baby with the bath water.

This book is not a representation of any one religious point of view. Rather, it looks at commonalities of faith among all who profess spiritual devotion and experience any degree of miraculous power. As with any teaching, the reader should allow the light within them to guide them as to what is useful and what is not in their personal journey with God.

I have laid out the book in a way to lead the reader through an understanding of the obstacles to exercising faith as a principle of power, namely in the subconscious blocks we have. In traditional Christian terminology, we might term these blocks as "sin," or that which appears to separate us from more fully accessing the love and power of God.

After gaining a basic understanding of those blocks that prevent most of us from accessing faith with power, we continue through a series of chapters on different levels and methods of accessing and clearing subconscious blocks, starting with the foundation needed to use any clearing method: self-love. Self-love is the key that we turn to allow God's grace into our lives. Without it, we will judge ourselves too harshly and not allow God's grace as fully as he would like to give it.

Finally, the book discusses spiritual creation and ascension as byproducts of faith as a principle of power, and how this faith impacts the transition of the earth into its higher states. There is a discussion on the importance of spiritual guidance and how to be in an optimum state of flow. I end with reflections on how faith in Jesus transitions during this discovery process as well.

The best use of this book is to follow where the Spirit leads you. For some, that may be to read the chapters in sequential order. For others, that may be to read a paragraph here or there and skip the rest.

Chapters 2, 10, 11 and 12 contain the real message of the book which I hope those reading will have a chance to see and consider. Chapters 3 through 9 are "how-to" chapters, and the concluding chapters of the book are more refinement of understandings presented in chapter 12 regarding the connection between faith and ascension. Chapter 16 is the icing on the cake, taking our faith beyond our subconscious limitations.

To help the reader know what chapters are most relevant to their particular phase of learning, I have included a brief summary of each of the chapters:

Chapter 1. Miracles tells the story of one of the first healings I participated in with my daughter. It also discusses the types of miracles outside of healing being seen in many places around the world as well as how we can learn faith from others who do not share our religious beliefs.

Chapter 2. Power vs Force is the meat of the book. It discusses the subconscious motives behind our actions and the reasons we don't see more miracles. I recommend everyone who reads this book to read this chapter at a minimum.

Chapter 3. Love as the Power of Deep Transformation discusses the type of self-love we need to have in order to truly face our subconscious limitations. It is a great chapter for anyone wanting to experience deep and lasting transformation or also anyone who has ever needed to feel more self-acceptance.

Chapter 4. The World as a Mirror teaches how to use the world as a mirror to see our hidden subconscious limitations. This chapter is helpful to understand why our lives show up the way they do and lays the foundation on how changing our internal state of being can actually change the world around us.

Chapter 5. Listening to the Mirror teaches how to use the subconscious reflections we see in the world around us to better understand the personal guidance we receive from God. This chapter is helpful for anyone who has ever received guidance from God only to find that it didn't turn out the way they hoped or expected.

Chapter 6. Subconscious Streaming discusses one of the simplest methods to access beliefs in the subconscious and to start resolving them. This chapter is good for those just beginning to develop mindfulness of the subconscious and its role in their faith. It may also be a good review for those who are more advanced.

Chapter 7. Belief Work is a dense collection of methods to access the subconscious limiting beliefs. This chapter may be more suited to more advanced students seeking specialized learning in belief work, although even beginning students may get a few insights in just skimming through the section headings.

Chapter 8. Heart-Centered Awareness teaches a faster way to release our limiting beliefs. It discusses how to shift our state of awareness from the limitations of our body-mind into the light that is in all things and through all things. It is a form of deep change that bypasses the need for belief work or other logical analysis of the subconscious.

Chapter 9. Acceptance as the Common Element of Faith goes deeper into the philosophy of what creates the healing or the miracle behind the various healing modalities independent of religious belief or technique. This chapter is suited for the more advanced student who is looking for the common link between so many different approaches to healing and miracles.

Chapter 10. Faith-Based Creation teaches how we co-create with God what shows up in the world around us by what we put in our hearts. This chapter is recommended for anyone who is looking to use faith to change what is showing up in their lives. In addition to personal stories and examples, it contains basic principles for those new to the idea of manifestation as well as some more advanced content for those already experienced with faith-based creation.

Chapter 11. The Role of Faith in the World's Transition is for anyone who is worried about world events, apocalyptic scripture, end-time dreams/visions, or how the world will transition. Using biblical scripture, it teaches how the fear in the hearts of people from many world religions is actually creating the very thing they hope to avoid, and how the faith of a single person literally changes what will be.

Chapter 12. Application and Ascension teaches how the increase in miracles showing up in various religions and philosophies around the world is related to the changes coming in the earth. The common principles and theories behind ascension are discussed. The manner in which different world philosophies will need to be able to learn from each other in order for the earth to rise is also laid out. This chapter is for anyone interested in the changes taking place in our bodies, minds and the world around us.

Chapter 13. Inner Guidance is for anyone looking to deepen their understanding of how God communicates with us. Those who begin the path of ascension experience a change in their relationship with God going from children who obey every word without question to teenagers of God who are expected to use their intelligence increasingly as they progress to become more like Him.

Chapter 14. Faith in Grace discusses our fastest path of progression. What we plant in our heart is made so. Faith that our progression is through the grace of God and not through our own merits is one of the most powerful beliefs we can plant. We grow faster by letting go and allowing God than through all of our other efforts combined. Thus we see the reason we are saved by grace after all we can do, because it took all of our efforts to finally realize we can't do it, to let go and allow God.

Chapter 15. The Flow That Puts It All Together takes the seemingly separate ideas in this book and ties them together. When we start making modifications to the subconscious, it is painstakingly slow. We must convince the mind of what is there before we can let go. However, the deeper we go, we can start to flow in joy, taking joy in our present circumstances even before our deepest prayers have been answered. As we restore this faith to our lives, the changes within our own hearts and the world around us accelerate.

Chapter 16. The Revelation of Jesus Christ discusses the principle of the mirror with respect to Jesus. If the world around us reflects back to us different aspects of our subconscious self, what does Jesus reflect? After we release all of the fear, guilt, and shame that perfect love casts out, how does our connection to him change? What does the experience of coming into his presence reflect back to us?

Regardless of which chapters or sections call to you, the passages written are meant for reflection. Take it slow. Notice the thoughts that come up in response to each paragraph or sentence. It may be helpful to read with a notebook nearby. You will gain far more from this book by allowing it to lead you through your own internal reflection and clearing than you will by just speeding through its contents.

Also, at the end of some of the sections and chapters, there are suggested reflections. You do not need to do all of these, but they can help give you ideas of how to make better use of the content and to have a real shift while incorporating the ideas that Spirit is leading you to reflect on in greater depth.

CHAPTER

1

Miracles

"Daddy! I *know* you can heal me!" were the words my seven-year-old daughter yelled at me as she continued to wretch.

My daughter was very sick, her insides violently rebelling against her. She was in an incredible amount of pain, and I felt trapped in a tough situation. My wife had left the house very angry with me, implying that she would have to consider whether our marriage would make it through the night. And now my daughter was sick, I didn't have transportation, and I was stuck in an overcrowded camper that we used as a poor substitute for a house. I felt alone, abandoned by God after all of my exercise of faith.

I had done everything I knew to help her. I had given her a blessing; I had prayed over her. Even after a year of witnessing others perform healing miracles, I felt like I knew nothing in this situation. I tried it all and nothing was working. In that state, I broke down with the overall circumstances in my life and began to cry in front of my daughter. All she kept saying was, "Daddy, heal me! You can do it!"

I couldn't understand why she was so insistent. I had never really talked to her about my studies over the past year, which involved people who could work miracles. My faith in my own ability to pull it off was running low—after all, I already tried what I knew how to do.

It's funny how a Ph.D. can actually work against you when it comes to exercising faith. The knowledge of what can be done and what can't be done scientifically can form an imposing barrier nearly impossible to overcome.

With tears in my eyes, I told her, "I'm sorry, honey, but I can't." It was more than a statement of my lack of faith. It was symbolic of me failing her, failing my family, and failing my wife. It was an admission of defeat, of giving up.

This was when her tone of voice changed noticeably. Instead of the voice of a feeble little girl, she spoke with power and strength, "Daaad! Ask, and it shall be given!" I looked up. I heard in her voice the answer to not only her sickness but also the problems I was struggling with in my life at that time. It was not the voice of my daughter, but the voice of a being of light speaking through her innocent frame.

Even knowing that an angel was speaking to me through my daughter, I was unable to exercise much faith. But I was able to pull together that mustard seed necessary to offer one more prayer. It was a feeble prayer, but I was obedient.

"Father, please heal my daughter. I have tried everything, but you told me to ask and it would be given. In Jesus's name, amen."

I looked up, wondering what would happen. My daughter was still channeling the voice of the angel to guide me through. "Dad, that was nice, and I feel a little better—now try again."

I tried again, this time allowing myself to believe a little more. She responded, "I feel like there is a darkness around my heart, Dad." Curious now, I allowed my prayer to get more specific about the darkness around her heart. Afterward, she said, "Dad, the darkness has moved out of my heart now and is in my stomach." This time my prayer was directed towards her stomach. She said, "Now my stomach feels better, but I just feel empty."

By this point, my faith had increased substantially, and I asked that the love of God be given to her to fill her heart and soul. As soon as I finished my prayer, she literally threw the blanket off of her and leaped up from the bed where she had been lying, and said, "Dad, I feel great! Now let's eat; I'm hungry!"

Sometimes when we think of miracles, not just the tender mercies or synchronicities in life, but those true life-changing miracles, we think the day for them may have long since passed. It was only those holy individuals of old who had that kind of faith and power, or perhaps there are powerful miracles in our day, but they seem beyond our personal reach—they are the domain of others.

It is the nature of humankind to find reasons why faith does not work. It is the subconscious core of unresolved fears and hurts within the carnal/natural person that denies the possibility that we could experience those types of divine interventions in our lives. More than a million excuses exist to either discount the existence of power in today's world or to believe that only others can access that power.

These limiting beliefs include everything from "God only allows miracles in the most sacred and limited of circumstances," to "it isn't God's will," to "only men with a certain priesthood can work them," to any other excuse under the sun. Perhaps we even tried to exercise faith in the promises of God without ever truly understanding the foundations upon which faith as a principle of power is based. Feeling let down, we made up excuses for why God does not grant miracles in abundance in our day. Whatever the excuse or the reason behind it, it all adds up to the same thing: a complete denial that faith can work in our lives as it has for those of old.

A miracle is generally defined as that which occurs for which we have no rational explanation. There is no limit to the types of miracles that can occur. Although I gave an example of a physical healing in this chapter, there are many more types of miracles being performed in today's world. I have personally witnessed hundreds and heard of thousands more. I have also been blessed to be a participant in the unfolding of a number of miracles. I have not yet decided whether it is more exciting to see a miracle or to be at the center of one unfolding.

While healing was most certainly one of my primary focuses when I was first led to study miracles, I have seen so much more evidence of other types of miracles that

have been described in recent near-death exp
Some who have passed to the other side ha
vision men and women coming forth on the e
near future exercising the power of God in grea
changing the nature of matter, having the natural lifetime extended, opening portals to move from one place to another, communicating long distance without the need for technology, having access to knowledge to build beautiful buildings without ever having taken the engineering or math classes that would ordinarily give them that knowledge, conversing in vision or even face-to-face with God and angels, and so many more. It seems like anything that can be imagined has been seen in these near-death experiences, and many of these have matched the biblical descriptions of scenarios leading up to a change in the end times.

As amazing as each of these gifts sounds, I have discovered and witnessed that many of these gifts are currently being taught in some capacity or another in different locations around the world. I felt God leading me forth just to witness these things, almost as if I were a scientist recording data of which the rest of the world is still largely unaware. The beauty of being a scientist is that I don't have to understand what is happening; I just have to faithfully record it. Then, from a non-emotional place, I can try to understand what I have witnessed and make conjectures about how and why it works. More amazing still is that I, a left-brained, doubting Thomas, have experienced an increase of these gifts as well.

While I have heard many things about negative or dark miracles, my discovery is that the vast portion of miracles performed happen at the hands of men and women who are sincere and loving. Like so many doctors and nurses, ey may not understand the source of their power and knowledge, but they are diligent in that skill with which they have been granted. They have studied many years to develop that power and to use it to help others. And just like the power to heal in a hospital, this knowledge itself is neither good nor evil. It is the individual who lays hold upon that power who decides how to wield it and with what intention.

Remember the counsel of Christ in his parable of the wise servant who knew how to use the mammon of this world to his benefit. Christ admonished his disciples to make friends with the mammon of this world so they could do his work more efficiently. If this is true for money, then how much more true for the gifts of healing and other miracles? If we can make money work for our Lord, then how much more so can we make spiritual gifts work for him?

Just as I went to a university to study with many professors who were the best in the world at what they did, so too can we study with the professors of the science of consciousness and spiritual gifts. We are not going to them for their religious understanding or their moral stance any more than we would go to university professors of business or science for those things. Rather, we are going to learn that knowledge from them that can be employed in the service of our God. Just as I could see and appreciate the sincerity and life-long devotion in my professors to the pursuit of knowledge—and be thankful for what they taught me—let us not throw out the baby with the bathwater in our study of those sciences on spiritual gifts just because the teacher is not of our religious disposition.

I spent many years learning those physical sciences that would allow me to impact millions of people in the developing world through my scientific innovations. How much time might we spend to learn those spiritual technologies to change the direction of the world itself? Who better to answer the call to learn these gifts than the Christians who await the return of Christ? But pray; get your own answer. Is this even possible for you? What would Christ have you to do with your life? Sit on the sidelines, or join the game? You decide.

My witness to you is that if I have been able to experience these gifts in part, then so can you. In fact, there is a high degree of probability that you can learn to apply many of these gifts to a far greater degree than me or even from those I have studied under. With Christ, all things are possible.

What is taught in part is not a limitation or a cap on what can be done by you as you apply faith. All that you see in the world is as a mirror, reflecting back to you not limitations, but a glimmer of your own infinite potential to be in the service of God and to unfold greater works upon this earth. Is that not what Christ said? Greater works than these shall we do if we but believe?

It is my hope that my descriptions of what has created the faith to produce miracles in the lives of others will be of benefit to you. I do not describe the miracles half so much as the faith itself and the techniques for developing that faith. If you want to read about miracles, there are plenty of books out there that discuss these. This book is for developing your faith so that you can have the changes of heart that lead to the experience of miracles. When you understand the foundations of faith as a principle of power and apply those foundations, the miracles will follow on their own.

CHAPTER

2

Power vs Force

One of the primary inhibitions in the development of faith as a principle of power is a lack of understanding of emotion in the human experience. We do not understand the process of grieving and healing. In the course of healing, there are a large number of emotions, some of which are taboo in our culture. In failing to see the necessity of certain emotional states in healing, we block the efforts of God to bring up those subconscious pains that most need healing.

For example, when a loved one is taken unexpectedly in the prime of their life, we may end up feeling a mixture of grief and even anger. Our anger may feel inappropriate, because it is directed at individuals we know are innocent, or even at God. Because of our fear of feeling this emotion, especially any anger directed at God, we may suppress the emotion rather than allowing it to surface for healing.

The greatest irony in this process is that often we block these emotions through a misguided belief that this is the way that God or our loved ones will accept us. We do not understand that God will not judge us for these emotions, but that it is often God himself who brings these emotions to our attention for love and healing. Suppressing them by pretending that we do not experience these emotions is a form of damming the river, stopping the outpouring and healing of the soul before God.

To truly heal from our subconscious hurts, it can be very helpful to not only understand the different emotions involved but to see our subconscious strategies in avoiding these emotions. There needs to be a full, complete and even radical honesty with ourselves about what we are feeling and why. This takes courage. To face our own inner darkness takes a level of courage that few people possess in this life.

Perhaps this is also why few people ever progress to the point of working miracles. Even some of those who work miracles seem to simply be born with the gift. It is rare for an individual to understand and engage in the process of healing that will lead to that blessing in their family line as well. Although your family line may not have been blessed with the gifts of healing others, conversing with angels, looking into the heavens or other gifts too numerous to count, each of these gifts can be acquired to the extent you are willing to allow healing take place at the deepest levels of the subconscious. Once you open these gifts for you, you will place the seeds in your own lineage for others sharing your DNA to develop them more readily as well. In other words, you interrupt the chains of the past and create a new path of possibility for you and your posterity.

So, we start with an effort to understand the individual emotions. We rank them, not to judge them, but to help the conscious mind understand the progression and comprehend the strategies of avoidance. By understanding the individual emotions and learning to see ourselves more in the way that God does, we can let go of our fear of experiencing certain emotional states, and allow them to flow through us more seamlessly. When emotions no longer get stuck, it allows for greater healing to take place. When we see emotions not as a judgment from God, but as his love upon us to bring our hurts to the surface for healing, then it becomes easier to allow these states to move through us without resistance.

Author and psychiatrist David R. Hawkins put together a scale of emotions to help people understand the stages of healing of the soul or spirit. Becoming familiar with what they are and our resistance to them can help us better understand faith as a principle of action and as a principle of power. The following chart is an adaptation of his work that has been modified to reference levels of faith and action.

POWER VS FORCE CHART

	Emotion/State	Level	God View	Level of Faith	Action
Faith, Hope, Charity	Enlightenment	1000 - 700	Self	Faith as a Principle of Power	Submitting to God, Letting Go
	Peace	600	All-Being		
	Joy	540	One		
	Love	500	Loving		
	Reason	400	Wise		
	Acceptance	350	Merciful		
	Willingness	310	Inspiring		
	Neutrality	250	Enabling		
Force	Courage	200	Permitting	Faith as a Principle of Action	Fighting to Obtain
	Pride	175	Indifferent		
	Anger	150	Vengeful		
	Desire	125	Denying		
	Fear	100	Punitive	Despair, Hopelessness	Inaction
	Grief	75	Disdainful		
	Apathy	50	Condemning		
	Guilt	30	Vindictive		
	Shame	20	Despising		

-Adapted from David R. Hawkins, Power vs Force (1994)

The chart ranks the emotions on a scale of 20 to 1000. Again, the ranking is not to judge the emotions, but to help us understand them. This, in turn, allows us to recognize progress easier when it is made and to see our unconscious strategies of avoidance.

Shame is the lowest emotion on the chart and enlightenment is the highest state listed. There are a series of lines dividing different levels or classes of emotions. The lowest class includes the emotions of fear, guilt, and shame among others. These emotions are compulsory in nature. Often times, these lowest level emotions shut down faith and result in a state of inaction. A person feeling shame will believe that God has a very low view of them. In that state of shame, they will often not have enough will-power to even get out of bed in the morning. Their shame will lead them into a complete state of despair coupled with inaction. There is little to no faith in the conscious mind of a person who is experiencing shame.

The next series of emotions, including desire, anger, pride, and courage, are emotions of action. This level of emotion or higher is required for any action to be performed. While some of these emotions are seen as negative, they begin to convert the lower vibrational energies of fear, guilt, and shame into a form that can be acted upon. Thus, they are of a higher vibrational state.

Although the lowest emotions of force are associated with despair and inaction, when coupled with emotions of desire, anger, pride, and courage, they can help propel an individual into action using the classic carrot/stick approach. For example, a child who is refusing to do a school assignment may be offered the reward of a piece of candy (desire, level 125) along with the fear of punishment (fear, level 100) to help motivate them. This combination of emotions may create enough faith in the child to move them into the courage (level 200) to act and do their school assignment. This level of motivation, when applied to religious observation and spirituality, is insufficient to generate the power to work miracles and generally leads to a lower level of spirituality and joy in religious observance.

At the level of faith as a principle of action, the individual uses lower vibration emotions to try to control their behavior. The desire to obtain something or the pride in an outcome is leveraged against lower vibration emotions of fear, guilt, and shame to force or control behavior. The person is using force to try to control their environment. They are acting. They are doing. They consciously or unconsciously believe that the outcome is entirely or almost entirely based on their individual actions, whether physical, mental or emotional in nature. This is what characterizes faith as a principle of action. Ironically, in my experience in witnessing those who perform miracles consistently, these subconscious motivators are also one of the primary limitations to accessing faith as a principle of power.

For example, a father who is offering a prayer or blessing of healing for a sick child in the hospital may use all the right words. His actions are consistent with faith. But beneath his conscious view, the fear (level 100) of what will happen to his child if the blessing is not granted is what is actually driving his desire (level 125) for a healing to take place. This fear is based on his own shortcomings as a father, that his perceived negligence is somehow responsible for the injury his child now suffers from. If his child dies or is permanently crippled, he will bear the shame (level 20) of it and the weight of that responsibility. He fears he will be a failure in the eyes of his wife, his children, God and most of all, his own eyes.

Therefore, his desire for a miraculous healing for his child, which creates the faith-based action, in this case, is actually based on fear of his own unworthiness before God. It is as though all of his actions in requesting a blessing from God are actually a confession of his own unworthiness and a request from God to do the exact opposite of what he is pleading for. His subconscious is asking for judgment even while his conscious mind is looking for a miracle. With this inconsistency between mind and heart, there is no power. Therefore, even though the father's actions suggest faith, his subconscious motives underlying the actions are squashing the power of real belief.

This is not too different from the father who presented his child to Jesus to be healed. When Jesus told him that all things were possible to those who believed, the man responded, "Lord, I believe!" Jesus must have seen right through all the physical actions of this father into the heart of guilt that he carried, for then the man confessed his unbelief saying, "Help thou mine unbelief." (Mark 9:24)

Once the unbelief had been both seen and acknowledged honestly before God, the man then released his own responsibility to be fully worthy through his actions and used his agency to give his power back to God. This moment of deep honesty in acknowledging his weakness and letting go of the need to "earn" the healing himself took him from faith as a principle of action into faith as a principle of power, and his son was healed.

This leads us to the next tier of emotions that has to do with letting go and placing faith squarely in God. The person is no longer the doer, God is. The emotions at this level release the fight. They let go of the struggle, and a person enters into deeper levels of faith and submission. Just as there must be a seed of courage for there to be action, so must there also be a seed of acceptance for there to be power. This tier of emotions is connected with the miraculous as the sincere seeker of Christ learns to let go of their own will and allow God to take over.

Although we talk liberally about letting go and allowing God to take over, this is not a trite statement. It was more than the man saying to Christ, "Lord, I believe." It took actually took the man looking into his own heart and coming face to face with his own pain and unbelief. It took letting go of the outcome and putting faith back into the hands of God that no matter what happened, it would be right. This step of letting go is actually a concrete, definable, and most importantly, learnable action. It can be performed by anyone, man, woman or child. Anyone who learns to truly let go and not just go through the motions can see an increase in the miraculous in their lives.

The final stages of emotional healing and progress move an individual into states of peace, love, and joy. These are not the versions of peace, love, and joy we think about in the world, but represent that most sublime of feelings, even the pure love of Jesus Christ, or charity as Paul calls it. This is the attribute possessed by all who are sincere followers of Christ. Interestingly, these are also the fruits of the Holy Ghost (Gal 5:22-23). It is by this love that those around us shall know we are his disciples. Looking at the chart, what changes might it take in our heart and our subconscious motivations to have this gift continuously?

In our pursuit of the power to work miracles, we would do well to remember Paul's teachings that even with all spiritual gifts, we are as nothing without charity. With the power to prophecy, or move mountains, still, we are nothing without charity. For all things must fail except for this pure love. As the world transitions from its fallen state into a greater glory, as our most beautiful understandings of today are set aside for the truths Christ reveals tomorrow, it is this pure love that remains.

The most beautiful aspect of developing faith as a principle of power is that it is a step along the journey to developing real, Christ-like charity. This charity is more than just a feeling we have developed from extreme discipline. Rather, it is a feeling that originates inside of us because of who we are. There is no force inside or outside of us to bring it out. It just is. After all the junk is cleared away, it is what remains. We are children of light, children of a Father of Light. Thus we are light. Without compulsory means, this love flows unto us forever and ever.

A little while back, there was a popular song, Fight Song, by Rachel Platten, that illustrates really well what emotions we access in our day to day lives and how we use them. Analyzing the chorus of this song using the emotions and their levels from the chart above we see:

This is my fight song
Anger 150, Pride 175

Take back my life song
Prove I'm alright song
Anger 150, Pride 175, Courage 200

My power's turned on
Starting right now I'll be strong
Pride 175, Courage 200

I'll play my fight song
Anger 150, Pride 175, Courage 200

And I don't really care if nobody else believes
'Cause I've still got a lot of fight left in me
Grief 75, Anger 150, Pride 175, Courage 200

The opening line of the chorus to this song starts with anger and pride. Why? The next two lines reveal it: courage to act, to change her life and move forward. Here, anger and pride are being used to create faith as a principle of action, to get out of a bad situation and make things better. It is only in the last two lines that she finally reveals the subconscious motivation behind the anger and pride she is using to create action: grief. Her statement "I don't really care" is actually a statement made in opposition to her true subconscious feelings of hurt, grief, and rejection. Thus, the anger and pride are reactions to the real hurt and are being used to create faith as a principle of action.

This song is typical of the fallen or premillennial world, which I refer to in this work as the "telestial world." We use low vibration emotions to create feelings of desire, anger or pride, which in turn are used to create the courage to act. The better someone does this in the telestial world, the more successful they appear. The real dividers between people are 1) How good are they at converting the low vibration (<100) emotion into faith as a principle of action? 2) Do they use that faith for worldly or spiritual ambitions? These are the two levels of judgment we find in this world, one of success, and one of purpose.

In reality, all people are experiencing low vibration emotion, whether or not they use it as fuel for action. It is what creates the common thread in the telestial world: force. Low vibration emotion is the vibration of force or the appearance of force. Just like in this song, grief was a means of compelling action by leading to anger, pride, and courage to get out of the grief. Many people will unconsciously create situations of low vibration in order to compel themselves to act.

It is only at the higher levels of neutrality and acceptance that we enter into power through real and authentic choice. Choice is the authentic desire of the heart that remains when all physical, emotional, mental and spiritual compulsion is released. The problem is, we often fear what we would do without compulsion in these areas of our lives. And fear is the opposite of faith, hope, and charity.

Power is not only symbolic of choice, it is also a literal fruit of faith at higher vibrations. Faith as a principle of power is the mechanism by which God acts, by which things come into being without effort, and with a little tongue in cheek in this case, without fight. Just as it takes a seed of courage for there to be faith as a principle of action, so too does it take a seed of acceptance for there to be faith as a principle of power. Power comes into being when we use our agency to release the fight and judgment unto God. It is when we turn things over to him that we see power manifest spontaneously in our lives, often in the form of the seemingly miraculous. This is a big part of what Jesus meant when he said that he could of his own self do nothing (John 5:30).

But we cannot fool God, we have to truly let go of our own will and desires and move into a state of acceptance at both the conscious and subconscious levels. This is full, deep and complete repentance. This is complete childlike submission to God, complete yielding of the heart resulting in complete sanctification. It is real faith that changes the heart, not just lip service. When we have this higher vibration version of faith, we start to have power in our lives.

Here is a slightly modified version of the song that moves the energy closer to acceptance (350) and a state of mind in which faith as a principle of power is more readily accessed:

> This is my light song
> Let go my life song
> Turn unto Christ song
> My power's turned on
> Starting right now I see the dawn
> I'll play my light song
> All I really need is to trust and believe
> 'Cause I've let go of all the fight left in me

Agency and the Division between Light and Dark

Before this world, we understand that the division between light and dark happened when Lucifer proposed to take agency away from humankind. We suppose that the choice was already made to give humankind their agency, but that same division is being carried out on earth today. But, how does one actually take agency away from a person?

Many of us have heard children being pressured into participating in an activity they do not like respond to their parents, "You're taking away my agency!" But how is this possible? Any parent soon learns they cannot physically force a child to do anything. However, from the child's perspective, the fear of his father's angry outburst or the guilt over her mother's emotional meltdown provides more motivation than whips or guns. Even modern parenting manuals recognize this type of parenting as "coercive," or that which seeks to control the child's behavior through the use or threat of emotional force.

After the death of Christ, we observe through his disciples that not even the most brutal of deaths could truly deprive them of their agency. The fact is that agency is taken through our unresolved emotions. It is not the thing itself that controls us, rather the fear of it or the fear of shame in it that controls us. For example, it is not death that controls us, rather the fear of death.

Since Christ's apostles had released their fear of death through the love they came to know through him, they were no longer controlled by the threats of men and governments. They had also released their desire for the things or praise of this world. Without any unresolved emotional carrot or stick that could motivate them, they were completely free to follow the pure love of Jesus Christ. Without the emotional trigger inside of us, there is nothing that can control or force us in any way.

Therefore in the fight between good and evil, there is the appearance of an ongoing battle for control over our agency until we release the triggers that give others control over us. The triggers are the vulnerabilities and hurt within our soul that give the fiery darts of the adversary access to our most tender places. Therefore, true agency is found through the healing of these hurts and vulnerabilities through the atonement of Christ to the degree that we are emotionally at peace no matter what is happening in the world around us.

But since most of us with any spiritual background do not go around with large amounts of fear, guilt, and shame in our conscious mind, what does this have to do with us? A whole lot it turns out. At least if you believe that it is important to purify not only the conscious mind, but also the heart, or in other words, the deep beliefs of the subconscious. If it is the pure in heart who are Zion and who establish Zion, then we need to understand this a whole lot better than we currently do.

Conscious vs Subconscious

In the telestial world, almost all subconscious motivation is based on force. Although a spiritual person will try to maintain their conscious mind in higher states, it is through the subconscious use of force that they achieve and maintain those states. This is the reason that individuals and the world cannot move from the fallen world to the millennial or terrestrial state. Zion cannot be achieved through force, whether of the more obvious physical nature, or the more subtle subconscious nature. It can only be achieved through purification of the heart, the release of the lower vibration emotions and beliefs.

Therefore, almost all action in the telestial world is derived from force of one form or another. People in the telestial world simply draw distinctions in the use of force as to the outcome. In the world, are you overcome by despair, or do you have the courage and motivation to make something of yourself? In various religions, is your desire (level 125) leading you to seek after worldly things or after heavenly things? Is your pride (level 175) leading you to establish your value in spiritual things or in worldly things?

In this world, we use force at the subconscious level to motivate ourselves almost exclusively. If we decide that the subconscious motivation of force that leads us to "sin" is no longer what we need, then we adopt a stronger language of force to override it: punishment by God (note that a punitive view of God registers with a subconscious state of fear at level 100). The fear, guilt, and shame of being condemned by God can for most people provide a force strong enough to change any behavior. They need only accept this possibility deep enough into their subconscious to make it work. Of course, there needs to be a tiny belief in the possibility of God's mercy or love in order for the person to truly utilize the fear of punishment.

For example, a person who is only afraid of God's punishment without any hope in God's love or mercy will be like the slothful servant in the parable of the talents. Without the corresponding hope in the mercy and good-will of his master, fear overrode his willingness to act and he buried his talent. If he had been able to couple that fear with at least a particle of faith or hope that he would be rewarded or that his master would be merciful in the event of an honest mistake, then he could have used the fear to help motivate him to action. Our fear of the consequence is insufficient to motivate us, but when coupled with the hope of a more desirable state, such as the mercy of God, we have the power to change our lives to a better state.

Today, we recognize that addiction, whether to drugs, porn, electronics, food, work or any other thing, is one way of enslaving a person and virtually stripping them of all choice. But at a subconscious level, what exactly is addiction? It is most often desire on the surface covering a host of unresolved, subconscious fear, grief, guilt and shame. In order to be released from the addiction, a person can either use even greater fear, guilt and shame to coerce obedience (which is the most common approach), or they can face and heal some of the subconscious hurts behind the addiction. It is important to note that the societal norm of blaming or shaming people with addictions tends to reinforce the very hurts the addicts are avoiding through their addictive behavior. Loving and accepting them can give them the courage to face what they have been afraid to see.

Shame

Out of all the low vibrations, shame is the lowest of the low. Anyone experiencing shame will feel that they are in hell. This is because shame is the substance of any hell that people experience whether in this life or the next. Not even physical torture or fear or hopelessness can compare to the exquisite pain that comes with shame.

People will do anything to move out of low vibration emotions, but shame is by far the most intense. A person feeling shame will usually only stay in that state a short time before covering it up with other emotions. Rather than healing and releasing shame, most often a person will move into other low vibrational states, such as hopelessness.

From there, a person may stay in a state of hopelessness, where they feel powerless, like a victim. Often they will continue to move into other emotions to cover hopelessness. Anger, for example, is where a person moves out of the lowest vibration emotions into a state where they can finally act. While anger may not seem high vibration, it is high relative to the state of inaction contained in hopelessness or the state of crushing despair known as shame.

One of the problems with shame is that because it is the feeling of hell, our subconscious will generally classify any experience of this emotion as punishment. Surely there would be no reason for God to ever take us so deep into despair unless it were being used as a punishment. We may see God as being willing to *try* us, but never *punish* us unless we have been disobedient somewhere. The problem is that the feeling of shame is the same in both trials and punishment. It turns out that the difference between a trial and punishment is largely in the mind of the person experiencing the emotion.

An example of a trial is where an individual feels specifically guided by God to do something that would make them feel unusually vulnerable. But trusting in God, they step out into the open air only to find no support. To make matters worse, if the particular action committed is one associated with shame in their mind, they may feel betrayed by God. Since shame is equivalent to hell, which is punishment, then they have effectively been punished by God for exercising the most intense and vulnerable faith in their lives. It is easy to see that this state is not fun for anyone who experiences it.

The problem with associating any emotion as "punishment" or "darkness" is that it prevents us from experiencing the emotion, learning from it and healing what is deep inside of us. We do not understand all of the reasons we are present on earth, but whenever a low-vibration emotion surfaces there are at least two ways to view it: 1) Something undesirable to be suppressed so that we are not judged by God, ourselves, or others for it or 2) A deeply repressed part of us with which God finally trusts us enough to bring to the surface to be loved and healed.

When we consider the state of heaven we might think of a state of being where we would want to stay and abide forever. If we consider that it is the work of God to bring heaven down to earth, especially in the coming transition, then we might also wonder what ways of viewing the world we might hold in a state that endures forever. Would we prefer to 1) continually fight and judge every thought that arises within us and the world around us to avoid any possibility of the appearance of darkness or 2) see everything that arises as some part of us or God's creation that has yet to be seen, heard, or loved and is now arising so we can heal that part of ourselves that hurts?

In the former case, we are continuously judging and cutting off parts of the light of God from ourselves (remember that there is a light that is in all things and through all things of which Christ is a fullness). Christ did not separate himself from the prostitutes and sinners but loved them. How was he able to do this? By seeing the light that was in them. Whenever we love the light that is in another or exercise mercy unto another, we are doing the same unto ourselves.

If we truly understand this principle, then we will not fight against any emotion that arises. We will not see any emotion as beneath us, nor will we label it and judge it as evil or punishment for misdeeds. We will see that those emotions are rising within us so that we can be healed. Even the dread emotion of shame, the feeling of hell itself, is just another emotion that exists within the subconscious of every person in the fallen world and is waiting for us to develop enough charity to love it and heal it.

This is why it is essential for us to learn a form of self-charity if we are to ever develop the faith to work miracles with any consistency. Self-charity allows us to see the wounded places inside of ourselves and others that need healing. Rather than judging them, we embrace them with the salve of understanding, which in turn helps us to heal.

In one sense, if God trusts you enough to lead you into shame or other low-vibration suffering, he has loved you enough to heal you. It is as the touch of the surgeon's knife. Although it does not feel pleasant, it is the touch that can remove unseen cancer from within you.

When low vibration emotions surface within you, including shame, do your best to love that part of you that is afraid of the emotion. Do your best to love yourself in that state, to stay present with the emotion and not run from it or bury it. Exercise faith and hope that the only reason this or any other emotion surfaces is so that God can show you the places within you that still need healing. God reveals these without judgment; they are not punishment. Rather, they are simply shown so that we can see where God's love can have an even greater impact within us.

As we stay present with these emotions with courage, faith and hope that God will heal them, we will be rewarded with the fruits of understanding. Beyond understanding, we will develop long-suffering and compassion for others. This is a form of true humility when you can be present with your own greatest and deepest suffering without judgment. In this state, nothing can truly take you any lower. It becomes easy to be "real" with others by acknowledging your own faults and weaknesses. It becomes easy to love others because you have been willing to love yourself in that same state. When you no longer judge yourself for anything but freely allow the love of God to flow through to all of your faults and weaknesses, it becomes easy to provide the same courtesy to others. But as long as we pretend that we do not have faults and are unwilling to face our own greatest shames, we may continue to judge in others what we hate most about ourselves.

Can we transform our way of seeing the world so much that we can see the purpose in the suffering that God allowed in this world? This was no accident. All of these emotions, from the lowest to the highest, are present with purpose. We may not remember why we agreed to experience these emotions, but can we have enough faith and trust in God to submit as an infant in his arms to all things which come upon us? This state of complete surrender and trust (vibration > 200) is the beginning of the level of faith that produces miracles.

For your consideration:

- What emotions do you avoid at all cost? Remember, honesty here will lead to more healing than remaining in a state of denial. What hurts or feelings seem to control you?
- What would need to change in order for these emotions or feelings to be seen as blessings and gifts from God? Is that even possible?
- Do you believe that God truly loves you and that all things he provides for you are gifts? Or are some of life's events intended as punishments for you and others? Why do you see these as punishments instead of gifts of God's love? Is there anything from your past that might be contributing to this God-view?

Hopelessness and Other Impassable Walls of Personality or Emotion

When looking at a painting of a mountain, it appears to be a mountain from a distance. But upon closer examination, it dissolves into a complex layer of splotches of paint. The same can be said of our so-called personality (which we assume is unchangeable) and impassable walls of emotion. From a distance, they are a mountain, but upon closer examination, they dissolve into layers of splotches of low vibration emotion and beliefs.

The wall itself is almost always protecting a small part of ourselves that is hurt or afraid. Usually, it is so hurt or afraid that the wall is formed to keep us from even seeing it. Similar to the formation of scar tissue to wall off a section of you that the body does not know how to heal, so too is the formation of these emotional and spiritual scars.

We would think that these walls would be to protect us from the outside world, and that is true to an extent. But the greater reality is that the wall is to protect us from what we cannot bear to see, that which is so scary, so dark, or so hurtful that it would do unimaginable harm to address it.

So how do we get through a wall that was designed precisely for the reason that we don't want to see something? It is actually easier than you might think. But first, you need to let go and allow unconditional love into you for yourself.

You might think of having charity for yourself as being prideful, but note that on the chart love is at level 500 and pride is at level 175. Pride is actually the absence of real self-love. It is a cover for deeper hurts that have not been truly loved. Real self-love is actually the answer for pride.

For example, a narcissist, whom we say loves only himself, is actually compensating for deep hurts, shames, and fears more so than exercising any real self-love. Digging into their subconscious, we might find that their behavior is covering the abuse they suffered as a child from a mom or dad who constantly said they would never amount to anything. Faced with constant rejection and humiliation, they compensated for and covered the deep hurt by becoming focused on themselves. However, narcissism is the opposite of self-love. Self-love includes the willingness to be present with our deep hurts and love the wounded areas, not avoid them through endless self-aggrandizement. It includes the self-compassion that we never received from friends or loved ones and that our soul is so desperately crying out for. It is healing in its nature, undoing the very patterns that created the narcissist.

Self-love is made easier by understanding that God loves himself perfectly. He has to have a level of self-love we cannot even comprehend to stay joyful while seven billion of his children are suffering on the earth. He does not need any attention or validation from an outside source in order to stay in a perfect state of joy.

It is easy to think of loving ourselves if we could have that complete confidence that we were perfect in every way. But how do we treat ourselves when we fall short of perfection and make mistakes, whether big or small? If it were possible for God to make a mistake, would he still love himself or would he condemn himself with unrelenting brutality? When you make a mistake, is your first reaction to embrace yourself as a little child who has fallen and gotten a little dirty? Or do you immediately start cycling through the words and emotions of self-condemnation and self-deprecation?

To become like God, we must learn to love ourselves as he loves himself. And only in this way can we truly learn to keep the second great commandment, to love others as ourselves. If we wish to embrace others in their weaknesses, then we must learn to embrace ourselves in that same state. If we wish to love others with unconditional Christ-like love, then we must do the same for ourselves. Imagine if we loved others to the degree that God is capable of loving himself. Is this not the fruits we see in the life and sacrifice of Jesus Christ?

If we can love ourselves as unconditionally as God loves us and as he loves himself, then we can entice the parts hidden behind our walls to come out and into our view for healing. Like frightened or ashamed little children, if we can show them enough love and unconditional acceptance, then they will have the courage to show themselves to us. First, start by recognizing the existence of a wall that you believe is impassible or that hurts or that you are simply too afraid to look at. Then move into it so that the wall can resolve into its individual hurts.

You can do this by taking some time to sit quietly in a place with no distractions. A place that helps direct your heart to God may help too. In this state, close your eyes and simply allow yourself to feel. What feels stuck? What is filling you with anger or agitation at the moment? What are you afraid of or where is that grief coming from? When you start to see or connect with the emotion, you will find the wall. The wall is the belief that a certain state cannot change or should not change. It is the state of the absence of faith and hope. It is the rigidity of the heart.

When you find the wall, don't try to do anything with it. Just try to stay with it and not run away screaming. Try to step outside of yourself as the person feeling the emotions and instead be the person witnessing the person feeling the emotion. Witness what it is like to feel the discomfort. As you look closer, you may start to see that the discomfort is not a wall at all; rather it is a combination of a large number of smaller emotions, often connected with many discrete events and lessons from our lives that have taken on the appearance of a wall.

When the wall is no longer a wall, but many separate and unorganized hurts or fears, you can move through it. Give yourself plenty of time to do this. Simply love the parts of you that are feeling or have felt these hurts and fears. Love the part of you that resists loving you or says angry or judgmental things. Exercise faith in God that he can reveal the real hurt that the wall is protecting. Once the real hurt is addressed, the wall will come down often on its own.

Allow yourself to ask the really hard questions, "What is this wall protecting me from? What is so scary or dark or hurtful that I would hide it like this?" Keep asking questions and sit in the silence with faith that God will reveal it to you. You will know it when you find it.

My wife, Jenn, used this principle with our six-year-old daughter who had an anxiety attack, literally shrieking and hollering every time she had to take a shower. Jenn thought it might have to do with a fear of putting her head under water. But as Jenn started to ask my daughter to feel into the emotion, my daughter remembered an experience where she went to a hot spring when she was very young and put her head under a small waterfall that was too hot, and it burned her. No one else knew about the experience because she was too young to really speak of it at the time, but it left a record in her subconscious that formed a completely impassable wall, preventing her from taking showers or putting any kind of water over her head thereafter.

After discovering this, my wife quickly had her think about pleasant feelings and associated those with being underwater. After many years of having panic attacks about taking a shower, my daughter was finally able to go into the shower and enjoy it.

If there is unbearable emotion, love the part of you that fears to experience the emotion. When you can feel your emotions fully without judging them or being afraid of them, they will flow through you more easily and quickly. They may roar like a lion, but their power will soon blow through and leave you in the calm state of healing afterward.

If you are having difficulty *feeling* love for yourself, you may need to define love at a more basic level. Love is what is left when we have released all other responses. In its simplest form, it is attention itself. Like the attention we give the crying newborn who will not be comforted, we can simply have the courage to be present with ourselves in our emotions and just be. If you cannot *feel* love for yourself or these parts of you, then simply step into them with the intention to be present with them. Simply give them your attention. Become conscious of them. God is love, and we are made in his image. God's attention is love and so is yours, even if it is still in an infantile state. It may not feel like love, but it is a starting point when you are beyond feeling.

If there is a belief connected with the emotion, then you may need to ask God for some new perspective on the belief. Simply ask questions and open your heart and your mind to receive the answers. The answers may come in the form of words, a feeling, an understanding or in many other ways. Allow it to come. Often a new understanding can release the entire hurt.

Often as you look for answers behind the wall, or look for understanding from God, there will be a pause. If you are not used to sitting with your own emotions or you have fear about God not answering your prayers, that silence can be very uncomfortable. Treat the discomfort of feeling your emotion in the same way that you would any other part of the wall. This is just more detail that holds the wall together and is the next element that needs to be understood and loved in order to move through the wall.

Take the time that is necessary. Often times when I hit a slow point in my own journey inward, I let go of what I was thinking about. I simply turn all of my thoughts to the light of God and my faith in Him. I allow myself to feel that trust that he is guiding me and will lead me to the answers behind the wall. Then I let go and just allow myself to sit in the silence until the next thought or emotion arises. Usually, after a few minutes, the answer will come. Sometimes, I will not get the answer in that sitting and will simply have to come back to it another day. I just trust that even having the courage to be with the emotions in my wall for just a few moments has already started things shifting. I planted the seed of faith and the results will follow in their due time.

Once you have felt and released the emotion, or come to a new understanding, ask God for a healing for past versions of you that suffered through life without this understanding. See yourself in those time periods as though you had the knowledge you have now. This is not to create judgment or regret, but to see the healing and feel the joy of that healing. This can assist with releasing more hurt that has been stored at deep levels.

For your consideration:

- What areas in your life feel hopeless or stuck with no possibility for change? Consider areas in your home life, work-life, political life, religious life or even just your personal spiritual progression.

- Relax, close your eyes, and let go of any fear of connecting with this emotion. See if you can feel where the rigidity or paralyzing emotion is at in your body and move into it with love. Just feel into it with no intention to change it, just to love and understand it. What do you notice?
- With your eyes closed, ask what is behind the wall, what is it really protecting you from. Again, feel into it with no desire to change it or judge it, just to love it and understand it. What do you notice?

Understanding Desire

Desire is used in this world for almost everything we want. Whether we desire worldly things or spiritual gifts and experiences, desire is one of the most powerful motivators in this world. Although we typically call the desire for spiritual things good, it is still a telestial motivator of force.

Desire is made of two parts, a negative state in the present connecting us to a positive state in the future. We use the negative charge in the present to link us or attach us to the positive state in the future. This gives us incredible motivation to move forward, like the classic carrot in front of a rabbit.

This may seem like a good idea until we realize that we subconsciously sabotage our joy in the present in order to create this attachment. This is why Buddha taught that attachment is the cause of all suffering in this world. If we use the tool of force that does not allow us to have joy until we reach a future state, even and especially if we use it at the subconscious level, then we will never have joy.

How many of us have had the experience of finally receiving what we wanted only to find that our joy then moves on to another topic? The compulsive use of the tool of attachment or desire will always place our joy on the horizon in front of us. We will forever be chasing that ever elusive and receding horizon.

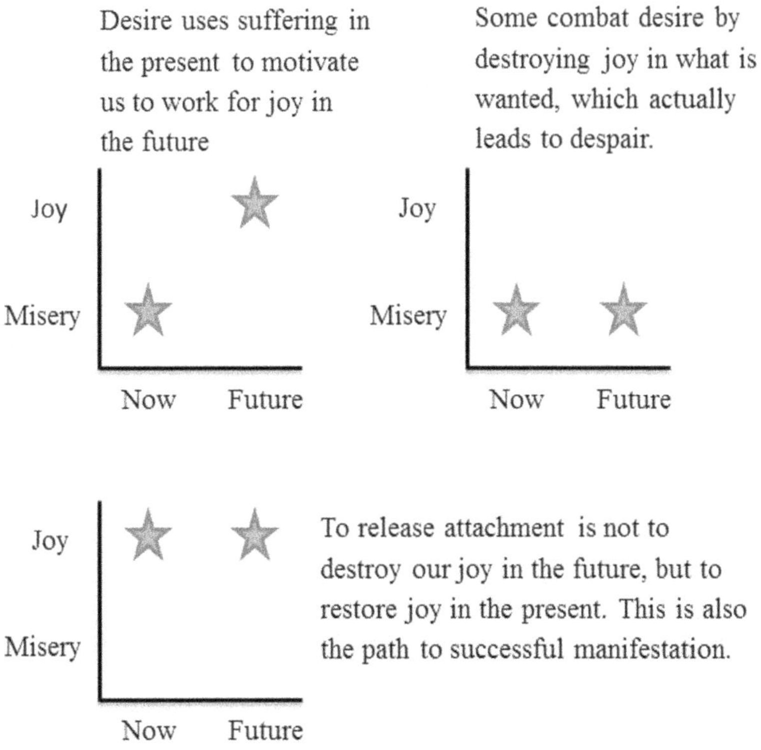

Figure 3

A spiritual seeker may eventually realize that desire is the root of much suffering. To combat it, they will often try to destroy the joy in the person or event they are attached to. This often has the result of producing depression, because we now have no joy in the present or in the future. This creates a state of hopelessness.

A better approach to releasing desire is to allow ourselves to have joy in the present. This requires allowing a lot of grace in our lives or a lot of time in meditation and reflection to understand the walls preventing us from having joy in the present. If we are successful in this approach, we will quickly shift ourselves into higher vibrational states of neutrality and acceptance (level 350).

An example of how desire works to compel us is in a single Christian woman who may want a family more than anything else in her life. She may feel incomplete without the blessings of a husband and children. She is "attached" to this God-given institution.

As day after day passes without an answer to her prayers to find that husband, she may eventually realize that this desire is making her miserable. She is unable to be happy in the present because of her attachment to this ideal.

To combat her attachment and try to be happy in the present, she may subconsciously try to destroy her desire in a number of ways. For example, she may remind herself of her friends who are married and constantly fighting, telling herself that marriage is no good anyway. She may tell herself that she is simply not cut out for marriage or that she was not meant for it in this life. She may even turn her back on her religion attributing its teachings as the cause of her suffering.

But out of all these choices, none of them addresses the real problem. Desire is a tool of force used to create action at the subconscious level by destroying our joy in the present in order to motivate us to move towards our objective. Destroying our happiness in that future objective will not make us happy in the present. Although it has the capacity to release us from the compulsion we feel at a subconscious level, it will end up making us miserable in the present and the future.

A better way to enter into a state of no force is by releasing the subconscious use of attachment to compel us forward. Many of our goals are joyful even without being compelled to do them. Marriage is a beautiful and worthwhile institution even without being forced into it by our subconscious!

Instead of destroying our joy in the present at the subconscious level to motivate us to action, what if we increased our joy in the present moment, giving our agency and power back to God? Then, instead of pining away about what we do not have in the present, we show the ultimate faith that God has already taken care of the details to our highest and greatest joy by being in a state of peace. We stop blaming ourselves for the failure to obtain what we want in the present moment and instead use our agency to put the ball back in God's court.

Interestingly, restoring joy in the present is both the means of ultimately obtaining what we want and releasing ourselves from unhealthy desires. An addict only maintains unhealthy desires by virtue of the hurt in the present. When the healing is done that allows the addict to find joy in the present moment, they will no longer desire their unhealthy addictions. Thus, restoring joy in the present is the key to not only having the faith to receive what we want but also to discern what our real joys are.

While neutrality and acceptance may not seem like a way to gain more of what we want in terms of spiritual states and experiences, it actually is. The faith exhibited to truly be in a state of neutrality and acceptance, to put the ball back into God's court, is one of power. Letting go of our "need" and putting our trust in God that he truly knows and understands our highest joy is faith indeed.

It is amazing how many of our desires are answered precisely when we let go of needing them. Is it any wonder that when we have both faith by letting go in the present and hope through our joy in the future that our prayers are more likely to be answered? It is when we let go of our desire and let God, that we return to emotional neutrality and acceptance in our natural state. This state of both faith and hope is where blessings flow. Our natural state with God is one of allowing what always and already is. We do not have to fight for spiritual experiences, they just are.

By relaxing the part of us that feels a need to fight and struggle, we actually allow more of the light and grace of Christ through. This healing use of our agency to let go and allow increases our faith and brings about more spiritual experiences and more of what we are seeking. Thus, with both an increase of faith in the present moment by letting go and a fullness of hope in the future, we are in an optimum state to be filled with the love and joy of God.

For your consideration:

- What material and spiritual desires do you have? Are you fully and truly happy in the present without them? What people, places, things, events, or experiences impact your level of happiness?

- Close your eyes, relax, and ask why your faith in Christ is not sufficient to have joy in the present even without these things. Keep asking questions until you feel like you have an understanding. Make a note of the answers for now.

Anger

We typically view anger as negative. But remember that even Christ allowed appropriate expression of anger and other emotions. Suppressing emotions does not allow them to be healed. Recognizing that when emotions surface, God is bringing them up to be seen and healed can help.

We also see anger surface when people leave their religion and anger surfaces in the form of resentment or other bitterness. This happens almost anytime an individual leaves one religion that had power in their lives and joins a new faith.

The purpose of anger is to move a person into action. To the extent that they were controlled in any degree at a conscious or unconscious level by fear, guilt, and shame, anger is one of the first levels of emotion that will allow a person to break out of that state and into action. For the person who moves from fear and guilt into anger, they have made a positive step forward.

For example, men and women who have lived an oppressed life under a cruel dictator might finally move from fear and shame into a state of active revolt through the use of anger. An abused child might take back their power and cease being a victim through anger. An individual no longer happy in a relationship might find a way out by making the other person wrong and incorporating anger. Anger allows a person in this situation to overlook the grief from losing any benefit they might have had in a relationship and take the steps they feel they need to in order to change what needs to be changed. Thus, anger is a useful tool that can lead us to necessary action in our lives.

Resentment is a special form of anger that helps protect us from falling back into a relationship again. This is true whether the relationship is with a person, idea or organization. For example, an individual feeling resentment towards a religious institution may be subconsciously trying to protect themselves from the hurt they felt in connection with that organization.

For those on the outside, this process can look counterproductive or even harmful. Those in a religion will often try to maintain their conscious mind in a state of faith or hope. When the conscious mind shifts to anger or bitterness, it appears like a shortcoming on the part of the person experiencing these emotions. What is not seen is the massive step forward the person may have taken by acknowledging their fear, grief or guilt and moving into a state of action.

The problem in our world surfaces when a person takes this step but is not fully aware of their subconscious programs nor do they have the tools to deal with them. Then they get stuck in anger and are unable to move on. At this point not only is their subconscious mind still full of fear, guilt, and shame, but their conscious mind becomes stuck in anger.

Being able to recognize anger as a reaction to other hurts that are buried deeper can help a person move through the wall and see the real problem. By finding and healing the real hurt, the individual can then progress again on their path to understanding God. Once the underlying hurt is addressed, then there is no more need for the subconscious mind to hold onto anger. Any anger or resentment is generally released with no further effort.

For your consideration:

- Make a list of resentments you have for any family members, friends, religious leaders, co-workers or even God. Remember, honesty will open the door to healing far faster than continued suppression and denial. It can be helpful to think of people from each phase of your life, early childhood, elementary school, middle school, high school, scouting events, marriage, etc. Include resentments toward ideas and organizations as well.
- For each resentment, close your eyes, relax, and ask "What is this protecting me from?"

Worldly and Spiritual Pride

Most of us would recognize worldly pride for what it is, a low vibration emotion. However, few of us can see the roots of spiritual pride.

Pride, when understood from a subconscious level, is any form of the statement, "I have value because..." Whatever we affix our value to becomes our pride. We have value by virtue of something we have which others do not. It is not in the comparison that we receive our value, but in the thing itself, which automatically elicits comparison. For many spiritual individuals, this means that their religious practice or their spiritual experiences can quickly form the basis for self-value and unconscious judgment of those around them.

For example, a person who goes to church every Sunday and observes all the commandments may feel a conscious or unconscious level of judgment for those who do not. Or perhaps they have a special loophole in their judgment for those who do not know any better, but for those who have been taught like themselves, there is a judgment. This judgment may arise completely unbidden regardless of how hard the individual tries to push it out of their mind and heart.

This judgment is often compensating for hurt in other areas. The individual sees others in the appearance of receiving blessings from God while not keeping the same commandments. There is an inner hurt from the burden of sacrifice needed to keep the commandment and a corresponding need to justify and maintain the courage to continue keeping the commandment. Therefore, the individual unconsciously places their value on the keeping of commandments, and by so doing robs others of any value who do not keep the commandments. This is where a large amount of our judgment comes from and is the reason it will not go away even though we know we should not judge.

This type of spiritual pride does not come from the love of keeping the commandment, but rather from the fear of not keeping the commandment. We subconsciously believe that if we released our value from these actions, we will no longer do them. When we finally move into the space of what this would mean about us if we did not keep the commandment or have the spiritual experiences we have, we are getting close to the underlying fears and hurts that keep us from progressing in our faith.

For many people of faith, and especially Christians, this is an unapproachable area. It is a blind spot in our faith, and it is the number one reason we are unable to see what keeps us from having a more powerful faith in God. The consequence of acknowledging what maintains our rigid obedience in Christ is too great to bear. We are too afraid of the result, what it would mean for us and our families. This is the heart of fear in the majority of Christians and consequently the root of Christian judgment towards others. It turns out that all judgment towards others is actually a judgment of self. As long as we are unwilling to see it or even consider it, then Christ cannot heal it. We must allow him in to receive the corresponding healing.

Interestingly, this is one of the major reasons why many non-Christians reject faith in Christ. They are sensitive to the energy of emotion and they feel the unconscious judgment coming from those who are called Christians. They see that the basis for faith in the majority of Christians is fear, guilt, and shame. They know that God is better than that. Hence, they throw the baby out with the bath water.

We as Christians can do better than that. It was Christ who taught us that the world would know us as his disciples by our love for one another. Note that it is not by our rigidity in obedience or evangelizing due to our subconscious fear, guilt, and shame that attracts them. Rather, it is our judgment-free love of one another because of the depth of healing we have experienced in Christ that allows them to finally see and recognize the truth. These observations are not judgments of our current state, but rather an invitation to know Christ more deeply and fully as he is, to heal from our inner hurt and finally know that joy that has been promised the saints.

While spiritual pride is a step forward from spiritual desire or anger in terms of a motivator, it is still a form of force and control. All it takes to bring someone with spiritual pride to their knees is to take away the thing that gives them value. What happens to a person whose value is in their flawless church attendance when they contract a chronic illness that prevents them from going anymore? What happens to the person who has the gift of communicating with angels when the angels stop coming or the information given is misinterpreted? They have a fatal flaw as it were. They are not in a state of humility because they can still be humbled by the loss of what gives them the appearance of their value.

Spiritual pride can be addressed the same as any other emotional wall. Rather than turning a blind eye to it, move into the wall, love it and seek for the source of hurt or fear behind the wall. Love it patiently and unconditionally until it dissolves.

For your consideration:

- What areas of your home, work, religious or other life give you value or pride in accomplishment? How would you feel about yourself or life in general if you no longer had those things or did those things? Is it possible that God loves you and values you even without them? Why are you unable to feel the same love and value for yourself that God feels for you?

- Is it possible that you could love and appreciate these actions, events or ideas even without making yourself spiritually vulnerable by placing your worth upon them? How would your life change as a result of that?
- Relax, close your eyes, and move into the hurt or feeling of rigidity that tells you it cannot be any other way. Release any fear, and be present with just the intention to love and understand the feeling. What do you notice? What is behind the feeling? What is it protecting you from?

Letting Go and Faith

Although letting go may seem to be the opposite of faith, it is actually the substance thereof. Clinging to what we want is not faith, rather it is fear that what we want will not be granted. Letting go such that we can sleep calmly and peacefully in the midst of the storm is faith. This is not a false, forced belief that we will have exactly what we want, but rather that whatever shows up is exactly what is needed. If it is different than what we have sought after, we allow the hope to rise up in our hearts that God has prepared something better for us than what we could have imagined, even if that something better may seem to hurt a little at first.

When God's people have had their hearts purified, it has almost always been as a result of their *yielding* their hearts to God. In other words, it is in submitting to God as a little child, having faith in all things that whatever happens is truly best, that the individual is sanctified and purified. This is the true form of repentance.

Repentance is more about the healing of the heart than it is a change in behavior. In a society which only knows and teaches faith as a principle of action, it should not be surprising that repentance is also taught as a series of steps or actions. While specific steps of recognizing our error or ceasing to do wrong can be signs of repentance, they are not repentance itself. Repentance is healing the hurt that led to an action whether or not the action itself is changed. This healing is typically connected with a change in understanding.

A person can change behavior without ever healing the hurts and incorrect beliefs that led to the behavior to begin with. Usually, when this is done, fear, guilt, and shame are used to suppress the behavior and the hurt that led to the behavior stays all the more neglected and unseen. Only by letting go and allowing the light of Christ to enter is the hurt truly healed which can then lead to a change in behavior spontaneously, without any effort at all.

The heart that has been fully healed will not only see the world differently, but it can look at all that has happened with gratitude. It can look upon all past action by self and others with a heart full of charity and love. There is no more separation of the present self from the past self's actions or from others. This state of letting go or acceptance is characterized by gratitude in all things. Thus, a complete transformation of the heart has not been received until we can view all things with gratitude.

Thus when we let go, it is more than a forced or false hope in the mind saying that we believe, it is composed of real feeling. But how do we achieve a real feeling without the use of force? It involves patience and letting go. It involves feeling into the source of the hurt that will not let us release. It involves seeing those parts of us that hurt or are afraid and simply being with them. We do not have to do anything. We need not change anything. We simply need to see them, to comprehend them, to love them. They will release in their own time when they are ready as we continue to open to the light of Christ and its healing effects. We simply need to exercise faith that it will happen at the perfect time in the perfect way, that there is nothing we can do to mess that process up.

It is also important to note that letting go is not another subconscious use of force. We may feel we are letting go as we push out negative emotions and thoughts. But in this case, we are often reacting to the negative emotion. It is our avoidance of hurt (eg fear) or our attempt to obtain (eg desire or maybe even pride) that is still driving us through subconscious motives of force; therefore, it is not truly letting go. Letting go actually moves us beyond force into power.

It may be difficult to imagine what you can do that is not a response to pain or other emotions of force, but it is actually simpler than you might realize. Imagine a place where you are at peace. For some that may be in a holy structure or temple. For others, that may be a place in nature or a place at home. For me, it is on a secluded seashore with the sound of the waves crashing in my ears, the warm salt air delicious in my nose and invigorating to my lungs, the cool spray of the waves in the breeze gently touching my skin. All of my senses are engaged and I find peace. It is a moment where I am truly content. I just want to be present with what I am experiencing in that moment. Everything else simply melts away.

Letting go is this feeling of spontaneous being that takes no effort. It is what we are when we are at rest. Letting go is about being present, not avoiding the present. There is no fight, no opposition, only peace. It was the Savior who said, "my peace I give unto you: not as the world giveth, give I unto you." (John 14:27) When we allow ourselves to truly rest in the peace of God, we are in a state of letting go. You can have this healing peace with you throughout your day. You need not wait for a moment of silence or formal prayer or meditation. It is available as often as we allow it, and it purifies us as often as we release into it.

Letting go can sometimes come in cycles as well. We may feel that we have obtained a joyful, loving state of consciousness. Nevertheless, it is God's intention to purify that which is already producing good fruit to where it can produce even more. Taking a step forward in this state can feel like taking a step backward. We thought we were done with shame and other low vibration emotions, but as soon as God undertakes to move us into greater understanding by enlarging our box, we have to deal with the subconscious terrain that had previously been outside of our view. Thus, letting go also includes allowing the cycle of expansion to continue by permitting God to move us through shame and other low vibration emotion long after we feel we should be done with these.

For your consideration:

- What storms are you facing in your life right now?
- Relax, close your eyes and just listen with love and an intention to understand. What is preventing you from letting go with the faith necessary to sleep in the middle of the storm?

- What is the worst thing that could happen if you just let go and trusted God? What is this fear protecting you from?
- What is the best thing that could happen if you just let go and trusted God? For this step, you might actually want to detail out the experience. With your eyes closed, imagine it. Feel it. Experience it. If you run into any objections, just ask what would be the best thing if it were possible? Be persistent and ask the question several times if need be. What would be the best thing about what you see? Keep going, this can be a fun exercise and incredibly helpful in letting go and building faith.

CHAPTER

3

Love as the Power of Deep Transformation

While faith is present in many forms and ways, those who consistently yield their hearts unto God find themselves purified in a way that connects them with a much deeper kind of faith. Their limitations are removed and they find they have the faith to move mountains.

Throughout this process, there is one unifying element to all of it, love. Love is the substance of divinity. It is the nature of God. In fact, John said, "God is love." God is not only love, he is light. In him, there is no darkness. In fact, He is the light that shines in the darkness. His light is found in all things and through all things, even in us. It is especially found in us, his children, who were made in his image.

This light that is in us, that we are made from, is itself love. We are love. For we were made in the image of God, and God is love. Can there be any other response from God for us than love? Given that he is love, are not all things then designed in love? Is not even the appearance of the discipline of the wayward child simply a loving action to bring that child back into the fold? Even the appearance of the greatest hell from God's point of view is nothing other than love.

Although it may be hard to see hardship and suffering as love from a kind and all-knowing God, we have this faith. Without faith that God is love we flounder in our lives. Those things that show up seem more like punishment, or cause us to question God's infallibility in some way. In these moments, it can be extremely difficult to trust that he is love, that what is showing up is truly an act of love.

Part of our difficulty is that we see through the eyes of the child who was frightened. No matter how loving or kind our caregivers were when we were children, there are remembrances of actions that were not perfectly God-like. Each of us carries the scars of childhood difficulty in our subconscious. These are moments where that innocent light of the newborn came face to face with the cold, hard realities of this world. In the face of those realities, our innocence retreated. We put walls up.

The walls we put up are to protect that innocence. Inside each of us is that newborn, precious and innocent still. We have simply hidden it over the years. We have tried to protect it. These walls and protection establish the roots of identity, or that which psychologists refer to as the ego.

The ego is not itself bad. Rather, it is the attempt to protect that innocence inside of us. Provoked by the world around us, it has grown inflamed and prevents any attempt to reach that purity within us. It is formed from the subconscious network of beliefs inherited from our ancestors and created from the world around us. It is the substance of the carnal/natural person, whose likeness has been described as an enemy of God. And why is it an enemy of God? Because it's only desire is to protect, it cannot feel into God's love in all things and through all things. Rather it exists as separate from God's love and reacts in inflamed ways to all that arises to protect the innocence within.

Our true inner nature is like a child who has been hurt, scarred and is afraid to come out. It hides in the closet, waiting for calmer and more rational minds to prevail. It waits for someone to come and love it, to be understood, to be protected. Most often, it is waiting for us to embrace ourselves the way that we have always wanted a parent to embrace us, to be loved the way we have always wanted a spouse to love us, to be understood the way we have always wanted to feel God's understanding for us. The interesting thing about this is that we are the only ones who can provide that embrace, that love, that understanding.

Although God is most certainly the fullness of love that we seek, we do not understand that we hold the key to receiving that love. God's love is always present. It is in all things and through all things, including in us. We are made from that love. If we cannot feel that love, why not? Is it because he is withholding it from us? Certainly not!

The only reason we cannot feel the love of God in every moment is that we subconsciously choose not to. We remain as separate. We are unwilling to love ourselves. We believe ourselves unworthy of love or only allowed love once we "earn" it. It is in these rare moments that we turn the key of self-love that we open the door to feeling God's love. Self-love is really just allowing ourselves to feel God's love. And God's love is what transforms and changes everything.

If you stop and think about it, what would cause you to change more? Feeling a thousand lashes from the adversary, or just one moment of the pure, unadulterated love of God? Part of this world's experience helps us to see that mountains of fear, guilt, and shame can never have as much power over us as one drop of the pure love of God. It is hope that changes us. And it is the love of God that produces faith, hope, and charity. We love because God first loved us.

So, when we self-love, we allow ourselves to feel the love of God which is always present with us. This is one of the reasons why letting go of judgment is so important. Every bit of judgment we have for those in the world around us is really a reflection of how we would judge ourselves in the same situation. The more intense the judgment of others, the more intense our own self-judgment. Judgment of any sort cuts us off from self-love in that area. Everywhere we fail to self-love, we fail to receive the healing love of God.

Sometimes we feel that self-love must be earned because that was our experience growing up or with the world around us. However, God is not like our parents. He is not like us. He is love. We will change far faster through feeling his love than by denying it to ourselves. A person who is loved fully and completely no longer has any need to sin. Sin is the reaction of an over-inflamed ego seeking for love in the deepest and most hurt places. When we love ourselves, we open to God's love and allow it to reach those places that are most vulnerable to what we see as sin. We release the charge as it were, and the need to sin dissolves with it.

If we want to reach the deepest, hurt places within us, we will not do it while we still retaining judgment for ourselves and others. We know that we no longer judge ourselves when we no longer hold any judgment for others. When we can forgive them as freely and lovingly as Christ did the woman taken in adultery, then we are in a state where we can forgive ourselves. Since our own judgment is what withholds the love of God for us, we can understand more fully the statement, judge not lest ye be judged.

The irony of all attempts to clear the subconscious of blocks to faith is that what our innocence is most afraid of is not the judgment of the world, it is our own judgment. Our innocence will remain in hiding until we can demonstrate that we will no longer judge its purity and light. Our ego will continue to roar and protect it until we can love in such a way that we no longer have a need for ego. In this way, the carnal/natural person within us is changed into a saint through the atonement of Christ.

Since our ego only exists to protect our innocence, and since our innocence most fears our own judgment, the action of releasing all judgment and loving all that arises within us becomes one of the most effective ways of dissolving ego. When there is nothing more to protect us from, the inflammation of the personality known as ego calms down. As the inflammation decreases, we begin to see with clearer eyes.

In terms of the emotions we described in the previous chapter, ego is a mix of worldly and spiritual desires, anger, pride, and courage. It is a protection from the fears, grief, hopelessness, guilt, and shame experienced at lower levels. It is largely the fear and judgment of these emotional states that give rise to ego as a protective mechanism. By loving all that is, even as God sees the purpose in all things and loves all things, we release that fear and hurt and the need for the ego to roar in order to protect us.

This action of opening ourselves to love more fully goes against our nature. It takes extreme courage and especially faith to do so. But the person who most needs that love is that innocent child within us. We will find that when we can love ourselves unconditionally, our ability to love others as Christ did increases.

It is in this state of unconditional love and acceptance of self that we will find our progress begins. It is at this point that our deepest nature will trust us enough to reveal the inner hurts that are in need of the most healing and love. This will seem painful at first because of the amount of hurt brought to our attention. But as we love it consistently and completely, we will find that God's love begins to penetrate our hearts and the healing we didn't even know we needed is administered fully and completely.

We are the agents of God's love. It is through our attention that we give it. Since God is love and we are made in his image, our very presence, our attention is love. Wherever we put our attention, we share that love. When we go inside of ourselves, it is just as important to be the emissary of that love as it would be in the world around us. Even when we fail to love ourselves, we can love that part of us that is hurting and refuses to love.

As we begin to see ourselves more in God's image, to see ourselves as love, we love all that arises whether internally or externally. We see everything that arises as the request from ourselves or the world around us to be loved more fully. Each emotion, each thought, each action within us and in those around us is just a request from a deep part of us to be loved. The good and the bad are all requests for more love from God.

Many, many parts of our subconscious will be brought to the surface as we love more fully and trust more fully that they are showing up not to punish or condemn us, but to bless us through deeper healing. The heavens do not want to cause us any more pain than is absolutely necessary for our growth. Therefore, if we see our subconscious hurts and flaws as condemnation, the heavens will be reluctant to bring them to the surface for healing. But if we can see all things within us with the acceptance and love of God's eyes, then the heavens will help us go through this deep healing much more quickly and easily. Just by being present with these deep parts of ourselves, by not withholding God's love from them by devotedly loving ourselves, the subconscious hurts often resolve on their own without any additional effort.

In the instances where deeper techniques are required for healing, love is still the substance of these more advanced techniques. With love as a foundation, we can begin to learn deeper and more effective ways of clearing our subconscious blocks to develop the faith that works miracles. Like a kindergarten class where the fundamentals are taught, love of all things that arise with a deep trust that everything that arises is geared towards our highest growth is the basis upon which we build. Having a deep grasp of the fundamentals will make it easier to learn and apply every other technique that follows.

For your consideration:

- Make a list of all the areas in your life, past and present, where you are angry, disappointed, or ashamed of yourself. Especially include any areas where you feel self-hatred or self-deprecation. Remember to be fully honest here. Close your eyes, relax and take a moment to imagine what it would be like if you loved yourself instead. Instead of whipping yourself into shape, imagine what your life would be like if you treated yourself the way God actually feels about you. How would you be different in that setting? What would change? What would stay the same?
- Does God hate you? Is He ashamed of you or disappointed in you in any way? Reflect on the statement that God is love. Why would you hold a view of God that is opposite of his nature? How is that helping you experience the opposite of heaven in this life? Why would you choose that viewpoint? What is it teaching you?
- Make a list of the people in your life who you wish would say something more loving or encouraging to you. Include family members, extended family, co-workers, people from church, neighbors, and others, including God. Open your heart and write what you wish each one would say to you. Now close your eyes, relax and imagine each one saying these things to you. How do you feel? Who is it that most needs to say these things and believe these things about you?

CHAPTER

4

The World as a Mirror

As we begin to see the world through the eyes of love and see how all things that arise are truly for our benefit, we open to the next idea or concept: The world is a mirror precisely calculated by God to reflect back to us our own deepest hurts that most need love and attention now. Although each person around us is having their own experience and is making their own choices, God is so incredibly efficient that the people and circumstances around us act as perfect mirrors. Like a surgeon's advanced 3-D imaging technology that precisely reveals where the operation is needed, the world is the most advanced 3-D imaging system ever. The events that show up in our lives mirror back to us exactly what needs to be loved and healed when it is ready to surface.

This idea may seem a little abstract at first, but notice the particular emotions that show up with the events in your life. How do you respond when your spouse comes home stressed and agitated? How do you feel when your children get in trouble at school? What is your reaction when your parents or friends criticize you? The physical events are not the reflections, rather they are the catalysts which bring deep emotion to the surface.

For example, when a man's wife is critical of the amount of time he spends with the family, what is this a reflection of? More likely than not, deep in his subconscious, he will find that he is inwardly critical of his own lack of attention to his family. Her criticism, rather than a demonstration of any shortcoming on his part, is really a reflection of how he feels deep inside. She is unconsciously acting as a mirror to reveal his deepest hurts so that they can be healed. Rather than a shortcoming, this is a blessing.

When a mother's children act out and behave contrary to all that she has taught them, what is this reflecting? One deep root to this could be the mother's own self-judgment for those very behaviors. There is a hurt inside of her that believes if she were to do those very things, she would be judged for them, that God would not love her. The children are unconsciously acting as mirrors to show their mother what her limitations on God's love are, and what her deepest fears are.

When a parent is deeply critical of you, what is this reflecting? What voices do you have playing out inside of you? Likely as not, you are playing a mirror for them in the same way they are for you. You are revealing to your parent those areas for which they judge themselves. They in return are showing you the criticism that you inherited from them or from the world. When you fail to listen to your own inner critical voice, the world is kind of enough to provide someone who will make us listen. This is not necessarily because you need to listen to those critical voices, but because the reflection shows you the hurt that needs to be healed—in this case, the tendency to be overly critical with yourself.

These physical events can be viewed in one of several ways. First, all negative events can be seen as temptations from the adversary trying to destroy your state of mind. Second, they can be seen as gifts from God to reveal places inside of you that are still hurt and need love and healing. If you resonate with the first way of seeing things, then you will always avoid negative events and will spend your life trying to suppress and distance yourself from the negative emotions that surface. If you resonate with the second viewpoint, then you will see all that arises as a gift from God. You will live in gratitude for everything that shows up.

Living in gratitude is a beautiful place to be. Interestingly, as you heal the deep hurts within you, there is a need for less and less physical disruption to mirror back to you the negative. Instead, what gets mirrored back to you is the positive that is arising within you. This can change what shows up in the world around you completely. With no more negative to reflect, the world begins to mirror back perfect love and acceptance. Even when difficult events arise, they are no longer seen as challenges, but as love itself.

This concept is found in the idea that perfect love casts out all fear. If we see the fear in the world around us, it is only because there is still fear in our hearts. When there is nothing but love left even in the deepest recesses of our heart, then all we see is love in the world around us, even in those actions that some might see as hurtful. Perfect love casts out all fear.

Take for example the evening news. What emotions does it bring up? Fear? Anger? Frustration? These emotions reveal the places inside you that feel powerless to change world events, that feel fear with life itself. The news, a neutral physical event, is then used to bring to mind those areas that most need healing. It reveals the charge that is still deep in your subconscious and is asking for healing.

Few people recognize the gift that mirrors are, however. Generally, we have not been educated about the subconscious and how to access and heal it. We feel like victims of events in the world around us. We never realize that it is not the events themselves that we fear, but the emotions we have attached to those events.

For a person who grows aware of their subconscious and heals the charge attached to the news, they could watch what shows up in a state of greater peace. This may lead to the person no longer needing the mirror of the news. They may cease to watch the news altogether. The types of news that show up when they are watching may change. Or the person may simply be in a state of peace that no longer reacts to what is being said or presented.

As wonderful as external events can be for revealing hurts that need healing, the greatest mirrors tend to be the ones found in the home, namely our families. Our parents, spouses, and children do an amazing job reflecting back to us our deepest hurts. It is often our spouses who agree to do the most reflecting.

As much as it is the choice of our spouse or children to engage in certain behavior, I have found it amazing the number of times changes in their behavior correspond with healing taking place in my subconscious. The minute that I heal the hurt that caused me to be frustrated with their behavior, they choose to behave differently. All the emotions of force in the world could not change them (eg complaining, guilting, shaming, etc), but then they suddenly decide to change on their own the minute I am healed and no longer need them to change.

As discussed before, the emotions of force are associated with faith as a principle of action. We take personal responsibility for trying to control the people and circumstances around us. There are many emotions of hurt, frustration, and failure that surface when our control breaks down. But when we move into a place of acceptance where we have let go of the hurt and the charge, then faith as a principle of power takes over. Behavior changes naturally and spontaneously, without force. Or in those cases where behavior does not change, we are no longer hurt by it.

It is not only those areas of negativity that are reflected in us but also those places of beauty. Take for instance the newborn. Any family that has a newborn come into their home has seen beauty in its most basic form. If you study the face and eyes of a newborn, you see a serenity, a sanctity that comes with them from above. Although they can do nothing for themselves and require effort from us to care for them, they are priceless. They are symbols of the innocence inside of each of us that needs do nothing or be nothing in order to be worthy of love. By holding and embracing them, we hold that part of us that is innocent and acknowledge its worth before God.

The beautiful thing about mirrors is that not only do they reflect back to us the good and the bad within us, they give us a chance to more intricately and more deeply love the unloved parts of ourselves. Each person or event that shows up in our space is acting as a mirror for a part of us that wants to be loved next. By embracing each person or event with the love that Christ had, we embrace those parts of ourselves and send healing more deeply into us.

How many of us have worn our lives out in the service of others? How many of us have burnt through all the capital in our figurative bank accounts of brotherly love and bankrupted ourselves in the name of Christ-like love? Did we not understand that by loving others we were, in fact, loving ourselves? Did we not understand that by loving others more deeply, we were filling those deepest holes within ourselves? If we can see ourselves in others, then we can fill our own need even as we fill the needs of others. Loving others becomes the means of finding healing for ourselves.

Think of God above. He loves us more than he loves himself. And yet, if he sees the part of us that is in him, then the more he loves us, the more he is filled with light. Also, look at his surroundings, what is reflected back to him on a continual basis? What state of joy must exist in his heart in order for such beautiful surroundings to be his reflection?

When Christ walked upon the earth, he saw himself in each of us. This is why we are told that the second great commandment is to love others as ourselves. We cannot truly fulfill this commandment without loving ourselves. If we loved ourselves as God loves us, then we would love all people as God loves us.

This is what allowed Christ to love so fully and so deeply and yet never deplete himself. He was always loving from a full tank, a full cup as it were. When we see in others the reflections of ourselves, we can love them more deeply, fully and authentically. We can love almost without ceasing or without tiring. Everything we give to them is returned to us in greater measure. It allows us to love others seemingly more than ourselves without ever depleting or neglecting our own cup.

Seeing past the blame that we place upon the world around us to its utility as a mirror is a way to grow in our ability to love and to heal. We cannot fully progress in our healing and in our faith until we learn to use the mirror of the world to a fuller degree. As long as we insist on seeing the world at the level of truth where it is a product of other people's agency we will stay in a state of blame where we deflect and avoid our own deepest hurts. The minute that we stop avoiding our own fears and hurts, and see that the world is a gift from God to help heal us of those deepest hurts, then we can release our state of being stuck in our progress and start to grow in leaps and bounds.

Imagine the change that could take place inside your own home if instead of blaming your spouse for the problems they are facing or appear to be creating if instead you embraced them and loved them as you would that part of you that is weak and in need of a hug? What if you stayed by their side in times of hurt or hardship and instead of hurting for them, sent more love to them and to you? When you can love those closest to you in their times of need such that you send love to both them and the place inside of you that hurts, you will be using the mirrors for what they are intended for.

The ability to see these mirrors and to acknowledge how God can use other people's agency in your life to reflect back your own hurts takes courage. More importantly, it takes self-love. If you are in a state of self-condemnation over any imperfection, however minor it may be, then you will have a harder time being honest with yourself about what that wayward child or fussy neighbor is truly reflecting. It takes honesty with one's self to see the truth. And it takes self-love to have the courage to be truly honest. Only in knowing that you can love and accept yourself no matter what shows up can you face the deepest hurts within you. When you are that loving and that honest, you will see the truth and the truth shall set you free.

For your consideration:

- Who are the mirrors in your life? Consider your spouse, children, parents, extended family, co-workers, friends, church leaders, authoritarian figures and others. Think about any person or situation that is causing you grief. Then relax, close your eyes and ask yourself what hurts are they reflecting or revealing in you? What are they showing you that still needs love and healing?
- As you find the hurt that needs love and healing, keep your eyes closed and move into the area that feels stuck without any need to change it. Simply let go of any fear of feeling it, and be present with it purely from the perspective of loving it and understanding it. What do you notice? Is this hurt protecting you from anything deeper?

CHAPTER

5

Listening to the Mirror

In Christian culture, we can become extremely rigid and focused on the will of God as it is given to us through certain forms of communication. For some Christians, we place all of our emphasis on the words of scripture. For others, we might place our faith entirely in the words of an authority figure from our religious life. And still others place their faith almost exclusively in the still small voice that comes through promptings of the Holy Ghost.

As individuals, we recognize one or more of these sources as the voice of God and we often see it as infallible. We put blinders on, as it were, reducing our vision to the one form of communication we recognize from God. Our limited understanding in this area can lead to extreme disappointment and the biggest trials of our faith if our expectations of God's voice to us are not fulfilled in every whit.

It is not that the voice of God is ever wrong, it is that our ability to connect with the voice of God and fully understand it is limited in this sphere. Even if we had the ability to truly hear it, we would not want to. If we knew the end from the beginning, it would spoil the very purpose for which we made our sojourn on this earth. This means that even in our best attempts to connect with what we see as the voice of God, we will be mistaken in some cases. Even Jesus did not know the end from the beginning. We are told that he grew from grace to grace.

The problem is we are taught to place all of our faith in God. We are taught to ignore the temptations and the waves of the world, so we intentionally tune out everything around us in an effort to cultivate faith and to please God. We do this by placing our faith in that one voice which we recognize as being God's voice. If that voice ever appears to fail us, it can lead us into the biggest trial of faith in our lives.

For a person who has placed their soul on the proverbial altar through faith in God's voice to them, they can feel severely betrayed and hurt if the words of God do not turn out exactly the way they expected. This is difficult because we know God cannot lie. We know God cannot make mistakes. So we immediately start to doubt our own connection with God. We start to doubt everything we learned. This process is one of the most intense refining fires a soul can traverse. This state is intensified with the magnitude of the spiritual experience and the amount of faith that was placed in it.

As I have pondered this state, I have noticed that most people of faith will sooner or later pass through this fiery trial. I have wondered how it is that we can be so full of faith, and yet so blind to what God's real intention is. What I have noticed is that we have a tendency to tune out the voices we think are less important than the voice we believe is God's. We are only seeing part of the picture. We see the voices of the world as either illusory in nature or deceptive. We are incapable of hearing them or learning from them.

But this assumes that the reflection in the world is of no value. While it is not the voice of God in an eternal sense, there is no waste in the reflection of the world around us. In fact, if we do not learn to use the mirror of the world, then we cannot truly hear what the voice of God is telling us.

If we see the world as strictly illusion or strictly deception, then we will place no value in the mirror. We place more value in the voice of God to us. Even then, there is a hierarchy to how we listen to the voice of God. We place more value on the voice of God to those who are authorities, and less value on those voices of God to those we view as subordinate to us by virtue of the priesthood they hold or by the nature and intensity of the spiritual experiences we have had. In any event, we do not see all voices of God as equal.

Because of this, we listen to some voices of God more than others. We are highly attuned to listen to voices of God in certain books more than others, in certain people more than others. We listen to the voice of God in certain frequencies of light more than others, for example, we may place ultimate value on the Holy Ghost. It is not that this is bad, but unless we hear the entire voice, we only getting a part of the message.

We do not realize for example, that God will speak by the power of the Holy Ghost to reveal our path of highest growth. What is not said by the Holy Ghost is that our path of highest growth will use the mirror of the world to show us what is in our hearts so that we can understand it and heal from it. While we may have thought that the voice of the Holy Ghost was giving us value for listening and following it in special ways, in reality, it was showing us our weakness so that we could heal our hurts.

If we are not aware of how to see and use the mirror of the world around us or if we place no value upon it because it is illusion or deception, then we will be blindsided by what happens next. In this case, we will assume that the word of God to us was whole or complete, and then when the world crumbles around us, we feel that we were lied to, betrayed or somehow deceived in our interaction with God. Yet, because it is impossible for God to lie or betray or deceive, we will enter into a potentially intense crisis of faith. All the while, we will not see that there is a pairing of God's voice through the Holy Ghost with his voice in other areas. The more powerful the revelation to us in the beginning and the more value we place in the nature of the spiritual experience (eg the more spiritual pride), the bigger the shockwave when we see the Lord's true purposes in what unfolded.

Even standing in the presence of God can be the setup for a much bigger fall because of the value we place on that experience. This event which we see as the epitome of our deliverance can, in fact, be the epitome of our spiritual pride, our inability to hear or see the world around us. To the extent that our spiritual experiences give us the feeling of being right or of not having to pay attention to the world due to its lesser value, no matter how beautiful those experience are or were, they will contribute to the depths of pain we feel when we come face to face with our reflection in the mirror.

It may be the Holy Ghost's job to lead us into all truth, but one of the ways the Holy Ghost leads us into truth is to use the mirror of the world. By giving us the direction that brings up our innermost thoughts, these are then reflected in the world around us which give us a chance for healing. If we do not understand this pairing of communication, then the intensity of the reflection in the world will oftentimes grow until we do pay attention to it, oftentimes with catastrophic outcomes.

Although we have been trained to place higher importance on some of the words of God to us than others, it would do us well to listen to the mirror. The mirror may not be the voice of God, but mirrors seldom lie. They can be distorted, but there is temporal truth in them. That truth is necessary for us to truly hear what it was that God was trying to tell us in the beginning. Was that instruction he gave us through the Holy Ghost, through our religious leaders, through scripture to get us to do something to succeed in that thing, or was it to get us to see a reflection of our deepest hurts and fears that would lead to healing?

It was Henry Eyring, a renowned physicist with faith in Christ, who observed that scientists were just reading the clues from God's scripture left in the annals of the earth's crust. While we seldom think of the world around us as scripture because of the erring nature of interpretation, it is God's creation. All things around us are reacting to and reflecting our state of being. God's words through the Holy Ghost do not stand alone. They are given in the midst of this world, in the midst of this mirror that was given to us for our good. Let us hear the voices of God that we are accustomed to, but then let us try them on in the mirror. By so doing, we will be listening to those words in context. We will better see why they were given and it is less likely we will be blindsided.

Like a two-year-old child that grows ever louder when ignored, the mirror of the world will grow increasingly incessant in its attempts to get our attention when we fail to see it. This is because God's objectives for us are not success in the way we view success. Rather, he desires our healing. If the world needs to grow crazy for a little while to get us to see, then so be it. All of creation is worth the cost of salvation for one of God's children.

So why can't God just come out and tell us this in his words to us? Why couldn't he just tell us what the purpose of the prompting was from the beginning? He could, but most of our learning here is experiential. We learn from experience, from seeing and incorporating truth. Certain truths have far more value to us when experienced than when taught in words. In fact, some truths cannot be understood at all until we experience them. This is especially the case where we are blind to the truth because of subconscious inheritance of cultural and societal beliefs.

If we understand God's purposes, then in a way, we already know that all things that are given are there to help us heal and find increased learning and understanding. This is God's success. His success is often our failure because, in the midst of our failure, we come face to face with the truths we have been ignoring. In seeing the truth, we are set free. We find the healing we have so desperately needed, that we never knew we were looking for.

Wouldn't it be marvelous though if we learned to read the signs of the times before they came to fruition? Wouldn't it be marvelous if we learned to listen to God not only in the Holy Ghost but in the mirror of the world around us? The fallen world is our schoolmaster. Until we have learned to heed our schoolmaster and understand the lessons we were sent here for, it will continue to dominate the course of our conversation. If it needs to elevate its voice through personal or worldwide catastrophes and calamities to get us to face our hurts and our fears, to move us into submission and yielding unto God, then it will. But then we ask ourselves the question, is it better to be compelled to be humble or to choose to be humble?

For your consideration:

- What are the ways God communicates with you? What do you recognize as his voice?
- What voices in the world around you are you currently deaf to or assign no value to? What are your blind spots?
- Reflect deeply on what is showing up around you that you have been ignoring. What are these things reflecting for you? How might those reflections change how you currently understand and interpret God's messages to you?

CHAPTER

6

Subconscious Streaming

Loving ourselves and the emotions that surface is wonderful, but how do we then access the deep areas of the subconscious? One of the easiest methods that can be done by yourself is the use of subconscious streaming. This is a technique for unfiltered, uncensored flow that gradually unravels a problem until the heart of it is found. This is used in talk therapy, but can also be used effectively simply by writing what comes to mind.

The technique is simple. Start with a piece of paper that can be burned when you are done or a blank document that can be deleted. Then write everything that comes to mind about the situation and what it feels like. As you do this, you will notice that certain items that you write are more sensitive than others. Write more about these areas that are more sensitive.

The net effect of this approach is to start leading you down a gradient towards the heart of the emotion that is responsible for the behavior or feeling at the surface. Keep in mind that the surface behavior or feelings are generally protecting you from what is at the bottom. The experience at the bottom is not always pleasant. The raw, uncensored thoughts may be inappropriate by society's standards. This is the reason why self-love is a necessary first step in order to move into this stage effectively.

A willingness to face anything that comes up, no matter how dark and scary is important. Sometimes it is helpful to consecrate the beginning of this activity with the prayer or intention that nothing that comes up is real. This is a form of acknowledging before God that you are going to look at the shadow portions of you, but that you want him to know and understand that these do not represent the true conscious feelings you hold. You are only bringing them up because you believe God wants you to bring them to light for healing.

The purpose of this acknowledgment is not to change God's viewpoint, rather it is to help us move past our own fear. If we fear that God will judge us for what comes to light, then we will not go deep enough to find the root. We will not address the real hurt or be that brutally honest. What if what comes up is an emotion of distrust in God? What if it is anger at God? Will we allow ourselves to acknowledge these things and to express it in its authentic language if we fear he will judge us? But if we understand that God wants us to see the *entire* emotion for what it is, to feel it and release it for healing purposes, then we can lovingly look at the one who feels these things. We can exercise the same love for this part of ourselves as God does.

Another fear that can come up is that if we acknowledge the shadow portion of ourselves, we will lose all moral restraint, that by somehow voicing it, it will become real. In a sense, this is correct. What we expose in our subconscious often does take on more shape. But the purpose in that is not one of darkness, it is one of healing. Guided by the light of Christ, we can take courage and move through the darkness into the healing we desire. By taking his hand, we can move forward in confidence without fear.

However, one of the greatest lies ever told about humanity is that at our heart we are dark. It is true that each of our subconscious programs in this fallen world pertains to survival and protection of that innocent part of us. However, beneath the subconscious programs, no matter how dark, is the heart of light that God gave us in the beginning.

This process is like uncovering layer upon layer of filthier dirt, only to find the treasure at the bottom. The treasure, in this case, is our pure, undefiled state. This beautiful innocence lays hidden within each of us. In the beginning, we were created in the image of God. Anything done to defile that image is at the surface level only. It may cause us and others around us to forget what we were, but at our heart, we are still that same child of God, full of light and all the potential in the world.

When we first start uncovering, we may feel fear in seeing how much dirt is in our subconscious. We may be afraid of the hurt or the raw feelings or the beliefs or the actions that are under there. If we stop at the fear, we will never reach understanding. We must press on to see why we are afraid of these things. Why do they hurt? When we love ourselves enough to sincerely listen to what is being said, we will get curious. When we get curious, we will ask questions to further increase the digging process.

While engaging in this process, it is wonderful to be connected to the light. The best way to dig into the subconscious is to have such a connection with God and angels that you can feel their whispers in your heart. Each of us possesses this ability or gift in different degrees. Some hear voices. Some see. Some simply have feelings. Some just know. Whatever that gift is that you have, it is important to connect with the light of God and to allow him to guide you. Even if you believe you do not have this gift at all, simply exercising the intention to connect with God and having the hope that whatever is exposed in you is brought up for healing can help. Every time we exercise faith in God, it is responded to, even if it is in subtle ways. Even the subtle answers can help in this process.

We can use this intention of faith in God in everything we do. We can exercise faith that all things that show up are geared towards our awakening into his light in greater and greater amounts. This allows us to roll with the events of life more fluidly and to see all things as beneficial to us. It allows us to greet each moment with more gratitude. This faith is answered by God too. It leads to the very awakening we have faith will come.

Consequently, when we use subconscious streaming through writing as a means of finding our deepest hurts and healing them, faith in God is a primary ingredient. Holding the belief in our hearts that God will use this not to condemn us, but to heal us really helps. Knowing that God is involved in the process, even if we cannot hear, feel or see him also helps. This allows us to have the courage to take the next step, to face the deepest emotions and hurts.

It is important to understand that when it is said that the conscious mind is just the tip of the iceberg, this is a true statement. You may feel that after digging on one or two issues, you will arrive at that covenanted pinnacle of perfection, or simply of perfect life harmony. You may be surprised to find that the subconscious is full of a seemingly endless stream of emotional hurts from which to heal.

Just like physical sickness seems to exhibit the same symptoms over and over again from hundreds of different viruses and bacteria, so too do some of our favorite physical and emotional symptoms stem from dozens if not hundreds of deep emotional and spiritual hurts. We may have the joy of uncovering and healing the same symptom over and over again in deeper and deeper layers of the subconscious in a seemingly never-ending process. Like a persistent weed, until we get the deepest roots, our issues will continue to resurface.

Despite all our best efforts to heal the subconscious, in the end, it is by grace that we are saved. It is by grace that the bulk of the work is done. Always allow room in your heart for faith in grace. In the end, this is the most important part of the clearing process.

As we dig down to the deepest emotions, we may find that we are overcome with raw emotion and the intensity of them. Once we find that deepest root where there are no more questions, no more curiosity, oftentimes it is enough to simply be with the emotion. In the past, we have run from this part of ourselves that hurt so much. By simply embracing it, facing it, no longer running from it, we are doing something that we have wanted from others more than anything. We are being present. We are listening. We are loving ourselves despite the deepest hurt or appearance of darkness. Just being present with the emotion and fully and sincerely allowing it to move through us is often enough to see the pattern change.

When we feel these deep emotions, we want to give the same amount of love and respect to ourselves that we would to a young child. We want to love these parts of ourselves unconditionally. That means, our purpose in being there is not to be the drill-sergeant parent to whip ourselves back into line. It is not to coax or manipulate that part of ourselves to no longer feel these things. It is to simply love ourselves as we are without the need for change. It is to give ourselves the one thing we never received from the world around us: unconditional acceptance and love.

For some, this might seem scary. Why would we change our behavior if we were unconditionally accepted the way we are? Wasn't it the disapproval of our parents about bad things and their doting over good things that taught us right from wrong? Shouldn't we disapprove of some things within ourselves? Without that lash of disapproval or the drive forward of the need for change, then how can we become better?

This goes back to the fundamental concepts in power versus force. In this fallen world, we have all learned to act using emotions of force. These include emotions that come with avoidance of parental disapproval contrasted with the desire for parental approval. The way we place our value in the approval of others, including God, is a big driver for us.

The problem is not the actions that these emotions produce, it is the force behind them. Our true nature is in the image of God. It does not need to be forced in order to move forward. Yes, force is sometimes required to overcome the other subconscious programs present in the physical bodies we received in this world, but when all the subconscious programs are cleared, what is real remains. And what is real is the pure love of God. It is light, for we are made in his image. We do not have to try to be good because we are good.

This enters into power, for when we are good not out of constraint or subconscious obligation, but because of the light that arises within us without any effort, we finally understand the meaning of the words of John: "...it doth not yet appear what we shall be: but we know that, when he shall appear, we shall be like him; for we shall see him as he is. And every man that hath this hope in him purifieth himself, even as he is pure." It is the hope that underneath all the subconscious programs, we are like him. It is from these negative programs and the belief that we are the sum of these programs that we seek salvation. It is the revelation of our true and inherent light that we seek from him, to know who and what we really are.

Therefore, when we arrive at the deepest emotions, we greet them with love. We know that they, like all things in our lives, only exist by permission from God. And God allows nothing to exist in our lives that is not ultimately for our good. Therefore, we can see these emotions not as darkness, but as servants of God designed to help us have the experience we came here to have. We can love them, express gratitude for them, and give them permission to resolve when they are ready or when they are done teaching us.

This state of emotion that I am describing is referred to as "acceptance." It is the doorway through which we must enter to arrive at the higher states of being. It is the state in which we have sincere faith that whatever is, is right. We see all things as God's servants to help lift, teach and raise us. It is the doorway to faith as a principle of power.

By entering into a state of acceptance with our deepest and darkest emotions, we release the charge that was holding them in place. This could be like a divorcee finally entering into a state of acceptance with the change in their understanding of God's plan for them and all the attendant drama and emotion corresponding to that change. In a state of acceptance, the charge, or deep emotion, on each of the memories and future possibilities is released. In place of the negative emotion formerly attached to each experience or thought, there is now acceptance, peace, understanding and even gratitude.

The presence of the charge is almost like an indicator telling the emotion or belief that we are not ready to release it. It is a sign that our schooling is not done. But just like in school, when we are done with our education, we put away the materials we had from our classes and we move into the rest of our lives. So too, when we are done with the education we are receiving, these emotions will move on.

In science, we learn that positive and negative charges attract each other. This type of ionic bond forms some of the strongest bonds known in chemistry. Only in the presence of a solvent that dissolves and stabilizes the charge can the positive and negative charge be separated. The solvent we apply here is love. It is joy. It is gratitude. When we can be grateful for all things that happen to us, it is like putting salt into water. The charges holding the salt together dissolve and the compound comes apart.

The fears and frustrations that cause your charge to stick to you can be dissolved in the light of Christ. They can be dissolved with the faith necessary to produce a child-like gratitude, a thankful heart for what is being experienced. Whether you are experiencing charge in the form of fear to face and feel an emotion, or pain because of what a loved one's criticism is suggesting, learning to deeply feel gratitude for all things that arise can release you from the pain formerly associated with the event and allow you to move into a space of light.

One of the fears we often face is, but what if this emotion persists for days or weeks or never goes away? That is a sincere fear. It is worth subconscious streaming in this area as well. Entering into acceptance means being able to love and accept ourselves even if the emotion does not clear or persists. It means having faith in God even if we do not find the power to change it within ourselves. It means letting go of the self-condemnation and being left with the trust that all will work out as it should.

Even better, it means having the faith necessary to be grateful for the limitations we are facing even if we do not presently know how God is using them to bless us. It is the inherent trust that he is blessing us, that all things, including our foibles and limitations, are gifts from God that we can only experience in this state of mortality and are expressions of love itself. The power of gratitude is one of letting go; it is the essence of true acceptance. Thus, gratitude has the power to open our hearts and release our incessant clutching when nothing else will.

When we have entered this state of acceptance, most of the emotions inside of us will move and change on their own accord. Again, when we are done with our schooling, then we can put the schooling materials away. The negative emotions exist to teach. When they are done teaching, we can dismiss them with gratitude for their service. We can dismiss them with love and understanding.

Sometimes as we reach those deepest levels of hurt within us, we desire to have more understanding. This can be an opportunity to ask God some sincere questions. If we have faith that he will answer, we will receive the answers. This may come through an understanding, it may come through a voice. However it comes, we will receive the answer we are sincerely seeking.

When we reach the bottom emotion and all we can do is acknowledge that our subconscious has a good point, this may be an indicator that more understanding would be beneficial for our journey. In this case, added knowledge about what we are struggling with can go a long way towards helping an individual release an emotion. Asking God for his perspective, for what we are missing can really help. How does he see what we are going through from his highest perspective? What is the principle of truth we are missing to combat the lie within us that is causing us so much pain?

The interesting thing about spiritual truth and spiritual forgery is that truth when unopposed, always brings feelings of light, of peace, hope, and joy. Even if something you find at the bottom of your subconscious appears true, if it is causing you pain, it means that there is something you are missing. The truth is being used as a whip in some way rather than as a salve. It is this misuse of the truth that you will want help in identifying. By seeing what has been causing the pain, it is easier to release. Once we see the truth, it will set us free.

When we are done learning from this exercise in subconscious streaming, we take the final step. In a symbol of releasing the emotion or beliefs behind our digging, we burn the paper we wrote on or delete the spreadsheet we were using. This allows us to use the physical as a means of telling our subconscious what we want to do with what we dug up: release it. Let it go.

When we do this, we allow our hearts to go through a spiritual rebirth of sorts. We can open our hearts with the intention of letting God and angels move whatever they need, to purify whatever they want. The fire is a symbol of the Holy Ghost and the purification that comes through cleansing by fire. We are in a way inviting the Spirit of God to enter into us and purify and sanctify us.

When this process is complete, it can leave you feeling many different ways. Most often, you will experience a feeling of neutrality, neither good nor bad. Occasionally, you will experience feelings of joy or sacredness as God helps you complete the process. Other times, you will still feel hurt. If this is the case, then you may have the opportunity to do another round of digging until you can sense a positive shift in your emotional state.

Remember that a positive state is not always entering into a state of bliss or joy. A positive shift is relative to what you were experiencing before. If you were in shame, then grief could be a positive shift. If you were in grief, then anger could be a positive shift. Wherever you shifted to is not the end of the journey. Rather it is the starting point for future clearing and learning.

For your consideration:

- Find a stuck point in your emotional or spiritual self. What isn't moving? With a prayer in your heart, start writing how it makes you feel. Write everything that comes to mind without censorship. If you find yourself judging what you are writing, write that. Follow the flow wherever it goes, including and especially if it leads to deep emotion. Keep going until you get to the point where the emotion stops.
- When you get to the point where the emotion stops, open your heart to God to learn something about your assumptions you didn't know before, to receive a new perspective, or to simply be in a state of acceptance for a few moments. Even if no new perspectives arise, just being with yourself in that sacred space following the emotion is a form of honoring and loving the innocence inside of you. Even this simple action will already start changing things in your life.

CHAPTER

7

Belief Work

Belief work is a slightly more advanced form of subconscious streaming. Rather than walking through all of the emotions in great detail, inspired questions are used to find the root more quickly. Also, in changing the belief, prayer or inspired intention are used to ask God to make the change. Each of these approaches has the potential to help accelerate the process of changing out the belief. Below are presented several types of questions to help identify the subconscious roots more quickly.

It is always helpful to start with the intention of connecting to the pure light of God, letting go of worries and moving into a place of possibilities before beginning. Start with a prayer to connect to the light, and then give time for the prayer to take effect by becoming aware of your breath. You might even allow your consciousness to drift as though on butterfly wings. Let visuals come into your mind of light. Try to imagine or feel what the pure light of God would feel like, especially in the absence of your filters.

For example, instead of limiting the light of God to what you think it is, let go of your expectations and allow it to surprise you. Allow it to teach you. If you can use visual based intention or prayer to move into resonance with this feeling your ability to dig and find the information you are seeking will be enhanced.

There are a number of intentions that you can carry when you connect with the pure light of God depending on how you understand that statement. That light could be seen as the Holy Spirit or even as the radiance emanating from the presence of God. Either of these is a good intention, but you will feel most connected if you consider that the pure light of God is the Intelligence that permeates all of existence of which Father and Christ are a fullness. They may have bodies, but they are also a fullness of this light.

It is into this pure, formless Intelligence that you want to connect and dissolve into. A simple prayer to connect with this pure light followed by closing your eyes and feeling as though you are moving through the universe into it will often dramatically change the way you feel. Allow your imagination to see it and bring the feeling into you. It is as though you lose your very identity and cease to exist as separate from that light for a moment. There is a change in how you see yourself from an individual separate from God to being the light that is inside of you that is in all things and through all things.

The use of visuals in prayer may surprise some, but even our own clichés tell us that a picture is worth a thousand words. If you feel like your prayers have hit a ceiling, then try incorporating visuals and emotions into the prayer to communicate more specifically what it is you are feeling and desiring in your interaction with God. God is far more intelligent than we are in our present state. He is more than capable of understanding all the languages of the world, including those languages of people without words. He can understand sign language and he can understand the meaning behind pictures.

Picturing what you want, sending the emotion that is coupled with that picture, can be a more effective form of prayer than words alone simply due to the volume of information contained in the intention. In fact, you can send information from other senses as well, such as taste, touch, smell or sound. The more you envision what you want by incorporating additional senses, the more specific you make it, the more emotion you will feel and the more real it becomes. Also, by incorporating emotion, we tend to align the mind and the heart. Those prayers in which our hearts are aligned with our minds tend to have much more substance and are responded to more readily.

Once you are relaxed and feel that you have connected to the light, you will be in a place to be inspired by the types of questions you are asking to open the subconscious more deeply. When you ask these questions, do not judge the answers. Rather, let the answers surface on their own. Let them surprise you. If you are surprised by the answer, or if the answer elicits strong emotion, you will know that you are on the right track. Example questions and when to use them are below.

For your consideration:

- Start by exercising the intention to connect to the pure light of God. Close your eyes, offer a silent prayer and follow the suggestions above. Make sure you are in a place where you can take your time with this with no interruptions. Often times, slowing your breathing and feeling as much reverence as possible will improve the experience. How do you feel? Is it any different than before trying this exercise?

- Following are nine different approaches to belief work to try. You will get the most out of this section if you pick areas from your life and apply each of these strategies:

Method #1: Opening the Mind to New Possibilities.

Sometimes the subconscious can become stuck with not knowing any other option. One of the easiest ways to dig is by looking at best case scenarios, rather than digging into the pain. To do this, simply ask what would be the best thing about having the opposite emotion or belief of whatever is being experienced. For example, if you are struggling with self-hatred, ask the question, "What would be the best thing if I loved myself?" Then take the answer to whatever unfiltered response arises and ask what the best thing would be about that. Keep going until you feel an emotional release. At the end, ask God to give you his perspective on having these understandings and feelings now. Open your heart and let go, giving yourself enough time to feel a change internally.

Sometimes during a digging session, you won't be able to find the best thing. You will have an objection, a doubt or some other inability to even imagine the best thing. Be honest about the objection. Then ask what would happen if that weren't the case. For example, you feel the best case isn't even possible. Simply counter with, "But what if it were possible, what would be the best thing about that?" Sometimes you will need to go through several layers of countering before you can visualize a best-case scenario. Be patient and stay with it.

Connecting to the pure light of God before digging will make it easier for you to let go of the doubts that prevent you from envisioning the best case scenario. It will also help you to feel the Spirit of God when you start looking at better creations. The Spirit will testify of truth, helping you to envision possibilities that you previously could not even consider. This will do more to change a heart in a moment than years of discussing the negative will ever do. Further, by thinking about positive outcomes in the Light, it will help you to start creating the very thing you are envisioning.

For best results, don't just imagine what the best case would look like. You need to actually put yourself into the situation and *feel* it. Describe the emotions to yourself in addition to envisioning what it looks like, smells like, tastes like, etc. It is the emotions that will help you to change the most and to create what you are envisioning. The other sensory perceptions will help you to connect with those positive emotions more easily.

Method #2: Identify How It Serves You.

This method is similar to the first method. However, instead of asking what the best thing would be about not having the belief, we ask what the best thing is about having the belief, or in other words, how the belief is serving you. If we understand anything about God, it is that He is amazingly efficient. There is no belief that we hold inside of ourselves that is not serving us somehow. In order to release the belief, it may be useful to know how the belief is serving us so that we can receive that same benefit in a less painful, more joyous way.

All beliefs we have serve us. Some people will be offended and say in great agitation, "There is absolutely nothing good about having this belief or condition!" In order to use the technique, you will need to understand that all beliefs serve us. There is nothing in our lives that we are not co-creating with God. Neither He nor we will allow ourselves to hang onto a belief that does not serve us in some way. It takes true courage to close our eyes and look deep to see how that pesky belief or situation is truly serving us.

The technique is exceedingly simple. Just ask, "What is the best thing about having this belief?" or alternatively, "How is this belief serving you?" When the answer comes, rephrase the answer and ask how that is serving you. Keep going with the questions until you reach an endpoint where the emotion or energy shifts. When you find out ultimately what benefit you are receiving from a particular belief or emotion, you can ask God to give you that benefit without the negative program. Ask him to reprogram your subconscious with how to have the benefit and what it would feel like to have it without the negativity.

Method #3: Clearing Fears.

Fears hold a lot of power of us. It may be that one of the primary mechanisms of maintaining the illusion of our separation from God (eg the veil) is through our fears. We are told that perfect love casts out all fear and are admonished to strip ourselves of our fears. While we are not often in conscious communication with our fears, many of our subconscious beliefs leading to our conscious behaviors are based on fear at their roots.

The easiest way to release the anchors that are fear based is to ask what would be the worst thing that could happen if you didn't have the belief (eg what would be the worst thing that could happen if you weren't afraid of the events leading up to the second coming?) Or alternatively, what would be the worst thing that could happen if the belief was true (eg what is the worst thing that could happen in the events leading up to the second coming?). Instead of running from the fear, go directly into the heart of it. Face it. Facing it and overcoming it in the mind is far better than having to face the fear in reality.

Each time you get an answer to the question, continue going deeper by asking what the worst thing would be about that. Proceed until 1) the emotion is too deep for you to go further 2) you find that you start circling around the same logic and are unable to go deeper 3) God tells you that you have gone deep enough.

If you become overwhelmed from emotion along the way, ask God to pull the trauma and emotion suffered from thinking about the experience so you can keep going and find the root. The probability of becoming emotional in this line of questioning is very high. The best thing you can do is to dig quickly, find the root and release it. Think about the efficiency of a doctor during open heart surgery. Keep your connection with God strong so that you can keep your focus on the purpose of what you are doing rather than being consumed by the emotion that is surfacing.

It is also helpful to remember you are not the emotion. Step out of the emotion and be the observer. Be the psychologist who is asking the part of you that hurts the questions, rather than the part that is feeling the pain.

In this type of digging death is not the end, and even hell is not necessarily an end. Confronting the worst fear is like going into the heart of a storm. At first, there is intense pain and trauma. Then you reach the calm after the storm. Everything has passed and all that remains are the lessons learned. Find the lessons at the end of the storm, even beyond death and hell where appropriate.

As an example, you have a fear of being alone. You fear being left by your spouse and those around you. Confronting this fear means allowing yourself to see it playing it out as though it were really happening. This will take you into the storm. Stay focused though and bring yourself through the storm by asking, "What happens next?" The crying stops and your subconscious responds more calmly and somewhat depressed, "I am all alone and I die." "Then what?" "I am alone in hell." "Ok, and what next?" Silence ensues while your subconscious is processing. "Wait a minute, I see a light." "What light is that?" "It's me discovering my own light in the midst of the darkness, a joy that can never be quenched." "So, why do I need to go into outer darkness to discover my own light?" "Because as long as there is darkness greater than what I have experienced, there will always be fear. I can only conquer fear once I have seen all the darkness." "But that is impossible to experience all the darkness; there is always a greater darkness. So what am I really learning from this impossible belief?" "That I cannot do it alone. I am learning to understand and accept the atonement of Jesus Christ." Then, you turn to God in prayer, "Father, please reprogram my subconscious beliefs showing me that I have already understood and accepted the atonement without needing to experience any more darkness. Please heal me from any emotional, mental or physical trauma I have suffered as a result of holding this belief. Thank you."

Every belief, no matter how seemingly horrid, carries with it lessons that were intended to be learned in this life. We came into this life to learn, and these beliefs that are in contradiction with our true nature and the nature of God help us to experience and learn. They create the bitter in our life that we might know the sweet. In order to change the beliefs, it is often helpful to understand the lessons that we have gained from having the beliefs and then ask God to help us have the lessons free from the negative belief (eg I know how to prepare by the Spirit for the Second Coming without being compelled to out of fear). Feel free to use inspiration during your prayer to cover more feelings that arise.

Method #4: Releasing Anger and Resentment.

Resentments are one of three "R" words that carry a lot of power: resentment, rejection, and regrets. Resentments almost always occur to keep us safe from a situation that caused us pain. As a part of anger, resentment is a slightly higher vibration emotion than grief or hopelessness and motivates us to action. Resentment as a specific type of anger usually motivates the type of action that prevents us from being hurt again. Resentments, rejection, and regrets will make it difficult for us to feel God's love or to see his power in our lives. Releasing these can bring a great deal of healing and relief for an individual.

In a relationship, there is seldom pure black or white. Despite any pain we may have felt with another, we will usually derive some benefit. We will feel a sort of love and connection. The pain of separation can be almost impossible for us to bear because of the benefits we derive. Therefore, separation becomes easier if we shift into anger by assigning a negative value to the other person. By making them evil or wrong in any way, we can move out of hopelessness into anger and from there into courage. Understanding how our subconscious uses anger to protect and motivate us is essential if we are to release our resentments. Releasing our resentments is part of the process of healing and reconnecting with our innermost hurts that most need to feel the love of God.

One of the easiest ways to dig on resentments or anger is to ask what the resentment is keeping us safe from. Once the cause of the resentment is discovered, digging can continue with any one of the other methods learned to this point. Upon finding the bottom belief, verify its presence by asking God if you have gone deep enough. Then ask God to replace it with the appropriate beliefs.

Use discernment on the timing of releasing a resentment. When resentments are released it should always be out of love and faith, and never out of force. Resentments that cannot be released without force, probably are not done being learned from yet. Simply love yourself in that state and have faith that the day for complete healing will arrive, and when it does, it will be beautiful. Until then, give gratitude for the protection that resentment provides you with. Love and appreciate that part of you that loves you enough to protect you in that way.

Method #5: Resolving Obligations/Commitments/Vows.

Obligations made at the subconscious level are semi-mandatory programs that can only be broken under extreme duress to ourselves and others around us. Energetic obligations can be entered into unconsciously during formal ceremonies, or even when our souls have that feeling of intense emotion that suggests, "I will never do that!" or "I will never forget this!" Breaking an energetic obligation even temporarily will cause serious psychological and emotional duress, like an irrational wall in an individual's personality that they are unable to cross even when others can plainly see the way through.

Energetic obligations are used throughout our experience in the telestial world to help us *always* do something. Like training wheels, they help us maintain a certain course, but at the expense of the greater flexibility of following the Spirit wherever it leads. Although many of the obligations we find in our subconscious were entered into with good intent, the irrational compulsion in an action rather than being free to choose to do something as directed by the Spirit ultimately restricts our joy.

In most instances of obligations, we will make the observation, "But that obligation is good, don't I want that?" Try to see the reasons why you made the obligation. This can be done easily by asking how the obligation is serving you. Once the root causes of making the obligation or commitment are understood, ask God to show your subconscious that you already have these lessons and know how to discern and follow the Spirit without being compelled to do so. This will generally resolve the obligation. However, in some instances, the obligation will need to be specifically "completed, resolved and sent to God's light" in order for it to dissipate.

Some individuals experienced a great deal of fear at early ages or inherited obligations from ancestors that were made in a great deal of fear. Fear-based obligations can be more persistent and take more work to release. Be patient and look for inspiration from God on how best to resolve these. ALL OBLIGATIONS CAN BE RELEASED. However, you will need to be sensitive to your own preparedness in releasing the obligation. Let God lead you in how much can be released. Pushing healing before an individual is ready can be harmful, like taking off a cast before the bone has set. Follow the instructions of Spirit in these areas.

Method #6: Origins.

In some digging sessions, it is extremely useful to find out where the belief came from. Asking questions such as who, what, when, where or why really help to get to the bottom. Some specific questions include "Who told this to me?" or "When was the first time I felt this way? Was that really the first time?" The purpose of these questions is to help you to step out of the problem set, to see that you are not the problem. Rather, the problem exists outside of the bounds with which you have defined it. When you can create space around a problem in your mind or subconscious, it gives room for answers you have not considered to present themselves. Everything we do in digging is to create room for faith, room for change.

Asking these types of questions will often take you into your childhood before the problems you are experiencing ever appeared. It will take you into your ancestry or even into experiences before this life. Remember your job is not to judge what is coming up, but to love all that arises, giving your subconscious self a safe place to express. With some childhood issues, you may need the help of a third party to see what is really there and resolve it.

When you find that place in time where something first happened, see what feelings were going on in your life at that time. What events were those feelings connected to and specifically what beliefs were tied to those feelings? This will help lead you to roots that you would have never imagined and that bring tremendous amounts of healing.

Once you find the roots, oftentimes it is helpful to not only pray for solutions for your present self, but also for the person you were at the time the events/feelings first happened. For example, you might ask that God's definition of safety be given to the two-year-old version of you and then let go and watch all the changes in your life that result from that time forward. This can help bring healing needed at that time into the present. You are addressing the part of you that was hurt and still is hurt, the child within you.

Method #7: Ask God.

In a number of cases when digging on especially difficult topics, you will get stuck on a belief. From your perspective, everything about the root belief seems right. You have simply reached a dead-end with no way out. In these cases, it can be very helpful to reconnect with the light and ask God's highest perspective on the subject. The deeper you are in the light, the easier it will be to hear God's voice or to feel the answers that come into your heart and mind. Having God's understanding of something can change our entire way of viewing the world and can resolve quite a few problems at the subconscious level. Once you have his perspective, ask him to reprogram your subconscious with that perspective and let go and allow any healing to take place.

Method #8: Deep Digging.

In some cases, especially when working on yourself, the emotions can become too personal and too intense to continue. It can be useful to reconnect to the light at that point and ask to interview the part of you that hurts. By interviewing the part that hurts or is afraid, you separate yourself from the intensity of the emotions. You are no longer the emotions, but the Intelligence that is understanding the part of you that is feeling the emotions.

Sometimes asking the part that is hurting results in no answer. If the part that is hurting feels that you will judge it in any way, or coerce it, then it can shut down and refuse to answer. Several things to consider or try are 1) Ask God for perfect charity for yourself and what it would feel like to fully listen to that part of you that hurts without any judgment. You might also try asking God for discernment in what to do. 2) Ask God why that part of you is not answering. Remove any blocks that show up or just keep asking God questions. Sometimes you can get all the information in a conversation with God. Once you have the information, ask God to pull any beliefs that are no longer useful and replace them with the inspired truth.

Another tool in deep digging is brainstorming. In this version of digging, start by finding the hurt. The hurt can either be found directly or by looking for the highest joy and seeing why that highest joy isn't being fulfilled. Then list as many different fears and/or beliefs connected to the hurt as possible. Keep going until you find one belief that seems to connect all the others. Then dig on this central belief. This can help you to more easily dig into the deeper layers rather than getting lost in dozens of surface beliefs. This is similar to pulling up a tree with all its branches by its roots rather than pruning off the branches one at a time. This will not work in every case, but in those where it does, it can bring the profound release of a lot of concerns with a minimal amount of effort.

Method #9: Be Inspired.

This method is really the best method to use. Rather than picking a single method and sticking with it doggedly, allow yourself to follow the flow of Spirit and light in what questions to ask. While you are first learning to dig this may seem difficult, but should become easier with practice and familiarity with the techniques. In the beginning, you can ask God which, if any, of the nine methods to use. As you gain more experience and comfort, you will simply ask the questions that pop into your mind, even and especially if they aren't a technique that was listed. You will learn to trust your intuition and will be guided to the most useful areas to dig on.

As you work on yourself, it is important to be able to keep the Spirit and your sense of curiosity. When you cease to see what is coming up as traumatic, but a journey into understanding God's purposes for everything you have experienced, you will have a natural curiosity that is mixed with a joyous sense of adventure. This curiosity will help you keep the Spirit. You will naturally be led to ask questions that lead quickly and easily to the deepest beliefs and bring healing to yourself and others. Remember that it is God that is doing the healing. He will direct you if you can just have a particle of faith in Him.

Sometimes there is discomfort in a digging session because it takes a while to receive an answer to a question you asked or you have no idea what to do next. Remember that you are not the one that is truly working on yourself. God is. He will provide you with the questions you need when you need them. Be comfortable with the pause. Oftentimes the pause is for you to process information so that you will be ready for the next question.

Also, the most important part of this entire process is the letting go. Asking the questions, finding the root cause behind the hurt and asking God to provide healing are all part of the process to help us let go. But in the end, none of this matters except for the degree to which we let go and allow God to enter into us. It is the changes he makes when we let go of the need to do it ourselves that matter.

When we let go, there is a feeling of release of emotion, a release of thought, a release of control over the situation. There is a simple trust in God and the outcome. Thus, even in belief work, we are using faith as a principle of power to affect the change. The practice of letting go we receive in belief work can carry to other areas of our lives where we learn to use faith as a principle of power.

None of the change that we receive from these techniques comes from the technique itself. The technique is simply the excuse our conscious mind uses to let go or to give ourselves permission to receive change from God. The understanding we receive is what gives our conscious mind permission to let go and allow God to change us. It is the reason or the logic that justifies the change. But in the end, all change is from grace. We are changed by grace to the degree that we allow ourselves to be.

CHAPTER

8

Heart-Centered Awareness

In life, rigidity is often seen as the limiting factor to joy. It is the dam that blocks the flow of light. As we start to become aware of the various emotions within us and as we release judgment upon them, our progress shifts to a place where we recognize flow. Spirit is fluid. It is not static. It is continuously moving, exploring, encouraging growth. When we are in the flow of Spirit, we are in light. We are in joy.

In the beginning, God created all things. Not only is God a physical personage of glorified flesh and bones, but he is also the embodiment of light. The light of God is in all things and through all things. It is the substance of creation, the Intelligence that gives life to all things. The physical personage of God is a fullness of this light, an embodiment of truth in all its forms.

When God created humankind, he created them in his own image. Just as God has a body combined with a fullness of light, so too do men and women have bodies with the potential for a fullness of light. As children of God, men and women have the potential to grow in wonderful and beautiful ways. This is what Jesus taught us as he grew from grace to grace, how we might progress to become like God by receiving more and more light until we have a fullness.

We find in our journey that those teachings that increase light within us are useful and good. Those that stifle light are less useful and possibly even detracting from our progression. If this is true with teachings, then how much more so with the emotional and mental states that we carry? Wherever there are blocks, no matter how seemingly benign, these blocks limit the flow of light. They limit our capacity to grow from grace to grace as Christ did.

The problem with our blocks is that we are often blind to them. We do not see them as blocks. Rather, we see them as self-evident facts of life, if we see them at all. But when we start to arrive at a level of emotional honesty with ourselves, we can start to feel where there is emotional or mental rigidity. Even as we can tell physically when there is a joint not moving well, so too can we perceive blocks at the emotional or mental level.

Many of our blocks and much of our rigidity comes from deep fear, guilt or shame. Patterns inherited from our own experiences, our parents, and ancestors, and from society at large form rigid boundaries that prevent us from seeing our infinite possibilities. Given our view of the world, we see through eyes of truth based on the patterns of the fallen world. But just like other truths of the fallen world, gravity, time and a multitude of physical laws, do not apply to the realms in which God lives, neither do our perceptions of truth bind or limit him. He is not an inmate of humanity's understanding or limitations. He is in a state of eternal flow. For us to be more like him, we must learn to release as he has released.

For some, letting go of rigidity can take on a monumental fear. It becomes tantamount to releasing their faith. Their rigidity and their faith go hand in hand because their relationship to God is largely through fear. The process of releasing faith as an outgrowth of fear and stepping into faith purely out of love is an overwhelming task for many. This is because there is a belief that the only thing that keeps a person safely on the path to God is fear itself. Thus fear is seen as our ally rather than our enemy.

In the telestial world, fear is our ally. It is what we have learned to use to conquer our own natures. Nevertheless, for progression into the state of faith which is of power, fear cannot come with us. Where Christ has gone, the carnal/natural person cannot go. We must learn to release the patterns and limitations of this mortal and fallen world. Perfect love casts out all fear, and God is perfect love. Therefore, there is no fear in heaven.

The world's version of faith, that faith which leads to action but has no power, uses fear to help motivate a person into action. At a secular level, this might mean using the fear of poverty to motivate better study habits, overcoming a tendency to procrastinate. On a religious level, it might mean leveraging the fear of punishment by God to help motivate more strict religious observance, overcoming moral laxness. In either case, this fear-based faith is a preparatory faith. It is not born of love. By nature of there being no fear in heaven, this type of faith which produces only action and no power does not exist in heaven.

Thus, to let go of fear is not to let go of faith, it is to embrace faith at an entirely new level. To believe that God will catch us when there is no more fear to govern us takes a level of faith that perhaps we have never before encountered in our lives. The same is true not only in our religious rigidity but in the rigidity we encounter in every area of our lives.

This is not to say that rigidity is bad or is not useful in some way. Rigidity has been used by many for thousands of years to maintain the ability to succeed in this world or to have moral fiber when the rest of the world does not. It is simply to say to the man or woman of God that if they desire to know God at a deeper level, then this is the next step.

We can recognize the presence of rigidity by the feeling of "I cannot even consider an alternative." There is often a feeling of fear, guilt or shame that accompanies the thought, reminding us that we cannot change. For example, a woman who is continuously criticized by her husband might feel stuck between her desire to have a voice and her need to fit the submissive image she believes is required to be a good Christian wife and to never cause any emotional disharmony in the home. Any thought of challenging his unrighteous dominion may produce feelings of fear, guilt or shame by running afoul of her view of what a good wife is. She cannot see that her definition of a "good wife" might be limiting. Nor can she see that the stuck feeling she has of her husband not being able to change is not allowing faith to flow. She is stuck on both sides.

The emotion that characterizes this state is one of rigidity. It is the feeling that no matter what, her husband cannot change. It is useless to even try. And that no matter what she feels, she cannot oppose him because to do so would violate her covenants with God. Although she is blaming God in a sense for not being able to change the situation, ironically, the problem is caused by not having the flexibility to see the bigger picture or the truth from God's vantage point. Consequently, rigidity can also be defined as the feeling of a loss of personal power or agency, anywhere where we feel like a victim and cannot change. Most frequently, it passes unrecognized because the rigidity is so ingrained within us, we do not even see it.

When we recognize rigidity and release it, we allow greater flow to return to our lives. Releasing rigidity is using our agency to give God permission to teach us something new. It is the recognition that God knows more than we do, that he is in control. It is a faith-based action because there is perfect trust and submission in the release of our deepest fears and shame. It is the act of letting go into the arms of God even and especially when we have been hurt and abused by letting go into others' arms.

Every time we exercise this perfect level of faith, every time we surrender unto God with the belief that he knows more than we do and is in control in a beautiful and harmonious way, we invite more light into our lives. We acknowledge that reality is not as solidly based on our perceptions as we once believed. We give room for the miraculous to occur. Thus, letting go is solidly integrated with the idea of the miraculous. It is the use of our agency to maintain our perception of the limitations on reality that prevent the miraculous from occurring.

Miracles can take place at many levels. It is not only in physical or emotional healing that we see miracles. But there can be rapid or even instantaneous changes in the world around us. We can have the heavens parted to see beautiful visions. Our understanding can be enlarged. The perspectives that were holding us back can suddenly be infused with new light and understanding, allowing us to take a step forward.

But how exactly do we let go? Letting go is not simply a statement. How often have we been told by others after experiencing an emotional slight or trauma to simply let it go? Without understanding how to do so, this is like pouring salt on a wound.

One of the best ways to let go is through heart-centered awareness. In heart-centered awareness, the person shifts their conscious mind spatially to a center point just behind and below the center of the chest. This can be done by incorporating visual intention with feeling. Remember that visual intention and feeling form the basis of prayer, but a form of prayer with more information. With the alignment of internal and external feelings, it can be a prayer with far more power than just the use of words.

The intention behind this visualization is to move our awareness from where we are fixated on the body and the problems we are having in this body, back to a point of reference where we exist as the light that is in all things and through all things. In a state where we exist as light, there are no problems. Further, there is no separation from the solution and not just one solution, but an infinite spectrum of solutions. To be in this space is to shift our frame of reference for reality.

When successfully done, a person will enter into a state where there is no thought, no emotion, and no physical action. It is a state where we cease to be the one acting. It is simple enough to then incorporate the intention that by so entering that state, we are putting the ball back into the hands of God and allowing him to take over. We are releasing all of our need to be the doer or to wrestle with the problem in any way. We are releasing all appearance of limitation or rigidity and trusting that all with God is right.

It is not to say that the person ceases to be conscious or that the mind ceases to produce imagery, but that there is no longer any thought or feeling about the imagery. In fact, one can stay in this state until a feeling arises that whatever is to be done has happened or shifted. There is a calm and complete acceptance of the outcome, whatever that is.

The visual intention can be exercised in any of a number of ways. Something as simple as feeling yourself at the center of a marble in the head, which then rolls backward and falls down your neck, stopping in the center of the heart space can work wonders. Using an elevator in which you enter and descend below the heart can work too. Any visual that resonates with you can work. If you are not visually based, you can use feeling or other sensory methods to exercise the intention, and then let go.

One of my favorite visuals to move into this space resembles the free-falling trust exercise. I lean backward in a comfortable chair, completely relaxing and then let go. In my mind's eye, I see myself falling backward through my heart into a soft cloud made of the pure light of Christ. It is like letting go into his merciful arms, only in a free-fall without limits. There is no limit to how deeply I can fall into his arms and place my trust in him. The deeper I fall, the more of my limitations, boundaries, and beliefs I let go of. It is a way to simply free fall in his love for me and let him take over and do the rest.

Sometimes in the process of letting go, objections come up. One feeling we are trying to release by falling into the light can sometimes be blocked by another emotion or belief. Whatever arises is simply the next in line to be loved, acknowledged and released. Continue moving from one objection to another, honoring it, feeling into it, and then dropping into the light. When you have hit the final objection holding the entire pattern in place, the entire pattern will release.

Really, this process is about connection. In our mortal state, so many of our problems arise from the appearance of separation from God. We continually judge and separate from everything around us and especially that which displeases us inside of us. What if we reversed that? What if we connected to all that was inside of us and accepted it with God's unconditional love, no matter how painful to see? And then what if we connected that to Christ's light and the possibility of boundless change?

So many of the answers in our lives come through connection and not separation. The intention of connecting with the emotions that block us from faith and from letting go allows us to reconnect with what hurts inside of us. Then, by taking that state and free-falling into the light of Christ within us, we are adding the intention of connecting the hurt with God's infinite grace. Thus, we are connected with all parts necessary for healing: We connect our awareness to the hurt and then to the light of God, and then step back and watch what God does. We are creating space for miracles and for change. We are connecting with faith as a principle of power.

Again, it is important to emphasize that there be a state of acceptance of the hurt. If we cannot see it in gratitude for what it has brought us or others, then we may not be done with the lesson and it may not shift. When we are truly in a state of gratitude, then we no longer feel the same need for it to go. We can be neutral. When we are locked in battle with it, then we will most likely reinforce its existence. It is by perfect neutrality where we can see God's will being done with or without the change that we move into a state of power.

This process does not need to take long. In fact, in time, you may find that you are willing and able to release without having to move through objections. The need to be present with and acknowledge the objections is one more thing that can be let go.

In terms of doing it "right," understand that you cannot do it wrong. The key pieces are 1) the intention and 2) letting go. There is not a right place in or around the heart that will make it work better, except as defined by your own beliefs. The simple act to connect with your center where you exist as the pure light in God is sufficient.

The idea that you exist as the pure light of God at some level may be hard for some. Remember, however, that God's light is in all things and through all things including you. In creating you in his image, he created you with his same potential to become conscious of the light or Intelligence in all matter. This is the light that existed prior to creation, from which all of existence has its basis. It is by becoming aware of this light and recognizing your unity with it that you take the next step in waking up as his child. Remember that Christ prayed for us to realize that we are one with him as he is one with the Father and the Father is one with us. Again, remember that you can pray and ask what pieces of this information are useful for you and what should be left alone for the time being. Even correct information can be misleading if offered at the wrong time.

The usefulness of being able to move into heart-centered awareness is that 1) it provides an incredible means to learn to let go and 2) it acknowledges a deeper truth of who and what we are. When we step into the light, we are stepping into infinite possibilities. We are reminding ourselves that we are not the limitations of the body, whether physical, mental, emotional or spiritual. We are not our limitations. We are infinite potential with infinite solutions in front of us. Recognition of infinite possibilities is faith and stands in contrast to doubt which is the recognition of any number of limitations. Letting go by moving into the light of infinite possibilities is a perfect act of faith. All things are possible to him who believes and who will allow.

Letting go is in contrast to what we learned in the last couple of chapters. While learning to love ourselves and the emotions is part of our experience here, it is not the end. Learning to change the patterns that show up by digging into them and finding and understanding the roots is beautiful, but is not the end. Each of these methods, if not understood in a deeper context, reinforces the physical, emotional or mental limitations as being us.

The more we wrestle with our problems, the more we acknowledge them as real and hold them in place.

Real power comes not in fixing the color of our sweater, by loving the existing color, or by changing out the threads one at a time, but by recognizing the sweater is not us—it can be changed. In this case, our beliefs and our problems are the threads of the sweater. We can change it by remembering we are not our problems or our limitations. We are infinite light and potential. We remember that we are infinite light and potential when we fall backward into our heart, like falling into the loving arms and light of Christ, and we let go of everything.

Perhaps the idea of infinite potential is not clear. In elementary school, we were taught that an electron circles an atom in a circular orbit. As we get older, we learn that this model was incorrect, and we are shown electrons circling in a more three-dimensional fashion. Then we are shown electrons in spheres. In college, we may be taught that the electron exists anywhere in a more hourglass-like pattern. Once we arrive in graduate school, we are finally taught the truth that our minds were unable to handle as children: the electron does not exist as a particle at all except where we look for it; it actually exists as a cloud of infinite potential. There is no particle; there is only the illusion of a particle.

The electron exists in all places at all times. It is an idea. It is potential. It is power. However, our conscious mind can only track one of these possibilities at a time. Therefore, we limit the infinite potential of the electron. When the conscious mind observes the electron, it collapses the wave function reducing the electron's location to a single position. This is not its actual position, but the position tracked by our conscious mind that is aware of only a single outcome or possibility.

Like the electron, our own potential is infinite. However, we only observe one possibility based on the programs we carry inside of us. By letting go and falling back into the light, there is a remembrance on a certain level that we are infinite potential, that there are infinite possibilities that we have yet to see. We are not limited. We are not victims. We are powerful. God is in us. When we let go, God acts through us.

Our understanding of God and the world around us is like this model of the electron as well. What we were taught as children is not what we understand when we grow older. We may be taught simple models to help us understand, but then God invites us to experience him, to shed our intellectual skin so to speak. Our experience with God is not intended to be passive. We are here to have an experience, and his call to us is very active. When we fall into our hearts, we not only let go of our problems, but we also let go of our limitations in our capacity to understand and relate to God.

For clearing purposes where we open more deeply to the miraculous, setting aside a time every day to reconnect with light and to let go and allow God to change us at every level can be phenomenal. There is no greater experience that the sincere seeker of Christ can have than to open fully and completely to the faith to be reborn on a daily basis. Continuous, fluid rebirth is the path of the seeker. It is the path that leads to faith as a principle of power.

For your consideration:

- Try the exercises listed in this chapter. Start by being the marble in the center of your mind. Roll backward and fall down the spine into the space just behind and below your heart. This is more than just a visualization, you must actually be the marble and feel yourself falling into that space. What do you notice? Try a different visualization, like a waterslide flowing into your heart. What do you notice? Try getting into an elevator that descends into your heart. What do you notice? Try free falling backward into your heart into the light of Christ. What do you notice? Try your own method. Which method works best for you?
- Using the method that works best for you, drop into your heart space. You might pop back out a second later. You will know you popped back out the moment you have awareness again. As soon as you pop back out, drop back in. Do this for several minutes while consciously giving permission to God and angels to shift whatever needs to change in you, whether it is physical, emotional, spiritual or otherwise. After several minutes of this exercise, what do you notice? What feels different physically, emotionally, mentally, spiritually or otherwise?

CHAPTER

9

Acceptance as the Common Element of Faith

As I have traveled parts of the world and studied miracles, I have seen that there is no prohibition by God on the working of miracles based on religious practice or belief. This observation surprised me more than any other thing that I saw thereafter. It was not the miracles that surprised me, it was the fact that God caused his sun to rise on people of all religions. The one element that seemed to be necessary in order to work miracles was a level of faith that went beyond outward appearances and obedience to external performances and ordinances. Rather, this level of faith was one that penetrated deep into the subconscious workings of an individual and was present as a state of surrender and understanding; namely that God not only had the power to do the miracle, not only wanted to do the miracle, but that there was nothing for the individual to do other than let go and allow God to take over.

I wish to contrast two different approaches to help teach this principle. In addition to different religions and practices, I have studied with those who have developed "energy work" methods or in other words those who have learned to work with God's light in a way that miracles become common. I want to highlight two different approaches to energy work because of the abundance of miracles in these two methods and because they are polar opposites of each other, making it easier to identify the common elements that are essential to the working of miracles.

The first of these energy modalities is called ThetaHealing developed by Vianna Stibal. It uses belief work to dig into the subconscious, identify the incorrect beliefs and replace them in order to see a change in the individual. Vianna seeks a form of God's light that seems to be consistent with the principle of Intelligence or the light that is in all things and through all things as experienced by individuals in near-death experiences. Vianna herself has had several near-death experiences.

In addition to teaching what she has learned, she also applies her method to heal others. At my last contact with her organization, she was only seeing stage four cancer patients with terminal cancer. Her clients were often not expected by the medical community to survive more than a week. She did not charge for her services with the individuals who she agreed to see. Complete healing of these individuals was not uncommon. To the client or the doctor seeing a follow-up MRI with no sign of cancer that was previously there, this could be considered either a "glitch" or something quite miraculous.

Vianna's method appeals slightly more to left brained people. There is a system of logic to it and the changes can be understood based on that logic. The method of Matrix Energetics developed by Richard Bartlett, on the other hand, is the polar opposite in its appeal to the right brain.

In contrast to Vianna's approach to connecting to the light in all things and through all things, Richard takes a heart-centered approach that is different in feeling. It seems to connect with the light of unorganized matter as a means of working miracles.

While some people may not know that matter is made of light, it is. Two photons of light can be combined to produce an electron and a positron, while an electron and a positron can be combined to produce two photons. Thus there are fundamentally two types of light: 1) Spiritual light or Intelligence and 2) the light of unorganized matter. Both emanate from God, like divine masculine and feminine energies that when combined produce life.

Vianna approaches healing from the left, while Richard approaches from the right. Vianna accesses a slower theta brainwave while Richard accesses a faster gamma brainwave. Vianna uses the masculine energy while Richard uses the feminine. They are polar opposites in their approach.

Instead of using a concrete system of logic, there is nothing logical about Matrix at all. Richard's approach to teaching is to continually bust the paradigms of all those present about what is actually responsible for the healing. His belief is that to define it in any way is to limit the power of the technique. It is through our subconscious definitions and reasons that we place on the success of it that we limit the power of God's expression through us.

Despite their differences, it is the similarities that are most interesting and serve to help delineate what opens the door to the faith that produces miracles. Richard claims that his secret is in "doing nothing," because he is not the doer. Vianna claims that her secret is simply being a "witness" to God. As with many explanations of individuals operating in the spiritual realms, the words point to the truth but can become limiting due to our limited understanding of words themselves. "Doing nothing" is not entirely correct. Richard is absolutely doing something that is connecting him with the divine. So is Vianna. Her statement of being a "witness" is also limiting.

Without experience and by placing our entire understanding based on what we comprehend of the words being used, we can be misled by our own filters. Being misled is not a bad thing, but will mean that we are incapable of accessing the power behind a technique to its fullest extent.

I asked Richard in a conference if he was just "witnessing" the event, if that was what he meant by "doing nothing." He responded that this was incorrect. Being a witness would imply that the individual was separate from what was occurring. Experiencing the event would also imply separation. By doing nothing, Richard means that he is releasing his need to do something, which is, in fact, a very powerful action. He is releasing all parts of the doer mentality from physical action, to thought, to emotional effort. There is no action. There is only the action of letting go all thought, feeling and physical action.

By one way of looking at it, he then becomes an observer or a witness. But because there is no thought, there is no observer. He enters into what could be described by some as a deep meditative state in which there is no separation of the individual from the light that is in all things and through all things. There is no identification of self as separate from other. In this state, he watches himself as the light do what is needed.

Although Vianna has a completely different logic and understanding, she too merges with the light. While Richard merges with the light of unorganized matter present in heart-centered awareness, Vianna merges with the light that is in all things and through all things. In so doing, she describes her action as being a witness. But here again, to witness implies separation. She speaks of the complete and total focus that is required for the duration of witnessing. It is my belief that she becomes the light even as Richard does, that she is no more a witness than he is. But in our vocabulary, the word witness is the closest thing she could find to describe what she is doing.

Although both Vianna and Richard have different visual experiences in their healing, Vianna often seeing medically significant imagery and Richard seeing sci-fi wormholes or other imagery which is nonsensical in nature, the visual imagery is not what defines the result. Rather, the allowance of the light to represent its action through imagery seems to be more of a focal point for the conscious mind to help it release the need for any thought or doer based action. All focal points can be considered as crutches or tools to help us access the state of mind needed for miracles. By allowing the focal point to appear using the imagery expected or desired by the participant, the conscious mind is able to enter a state of no thought more easily.

In my personal experience, we can specify the type of imagery that we would like the light to use in our experience with it. Even the nonsensical will have deep profundity when broken apart and analyzed in detail. But there is no need to understand the symbolism in order to experience the power of faith. Further, any attempt to force understanding of the symbolism is often a reactivation of the thought processes and can place limitations on what could be happening, which can inhibit the result in some cases.

While Richard enters through one door, Vianna enters through another. Both have different belief systems and sets of logic. Yet the door of letting go is the same for both. The power that is expressed through each only appears to be differentiated through their subconscious limitations in their own faith and rule sets in their respective techniques.

This can be understood with a Christian analogy. In the New Jerusalem described in scripture, there are twelve gates. It does not matter which of the twelve gates that you enter into as long as you ultimately arrive in the New Jerusalem. Likewise, for the performance of miracles, it does not appear to matter which gate of belief or technique you enter through so long as you arrive at the point of surrender to God. It is ultimately the faith of the individual to be able to release all need to do something and the subconscious limitations of that faith that seem to determine the outcome of any request for a miracle.

Once through one of the gates leading into the New Jerusalem, there is an integration of truth from each of the other gates in a state of unity in order to continue ascension or growth in God. It seems to be the same for the approach to healing work and miracles as well.

What this means for the aspiring Christian or frankly an individual from any other faith is that you can use your current religious beliefs to help you access miracles. There is no need to change religions in order to exercise faith as a principle of power. In fact, changing religious beliefs may trigger so much subconscious kick-back that it shuts down your ability to work miracles for quite some time.

Instead, all that is required is a willingness to examine the beliefs in the subconscious that prevent us from accessing that faith and a complete surrender unto God. Ultimately it is the surrender unto God free from subconscious limitations to faith that opens the door to power. In other words, if God allows the sincere faith of a non-religious individual to work miracles, then would he not also allow the faith of a Christian to work miracles? If prayer with faith in the universe is sufficient to activate miracles in a person with a clear subconscious, then should it not also work for an individual who offers prayers or blessings in the name of Christ, so long as they have purified their hearts and minds as well? The method is not the limiting factor, rather it is our faith and willingness to completely submit to God's will even into the subconscious layers of our being.

In fact, once we understand that the truths of the other gates can be used by God to bless lives, then we can incorporate those truths into our Christian understanding. It is my belief that our faith in Christ not only does not limit our potential but *enhances* it. When we learn to have faith to the degree and extent of some of our non-Christian brothers and sisters, then we will see the heavens open in truly miraculous ways. If they can have such profound results without Christ, then what can we accomplish with Him?

For your consideration:

- What elements do you believe are necessary for healing and other miracles to take place?
- Have a conversation with God, which of these elements are necessary for you to have the faith necessary to perform miracles and which are just training wheels helping you to reach a state of letting go? How does it help you to know the purpose of certain rituals is to assist you with letting go?

CHAPTER

10

Faith-Based Creation

The ability to create with faith as a principle of power stands in contrast to faith as a principle of action. Faith as a principle of action still uses subconscious motivators of force or control. Although we are trying to use them to accomplish "good" things, these motivators are a reflection of our agency that we must do it. By insisting that we do it, we use our agency to deny God the chance to simply give us the good gifts he desires for us out of the abundance of his love and mercy.

Faith as a principle of power involves letting go of the outcome and our overall control of it. We use our agency to give power back to God. By being in a state where our conscious and subconscious minds are in harmony and have truly let go, blessings flow in our lives without any effort at all. Anything we do is no longer to make it happen, but rather to follow the Spirit in those things that will bring us blessing and joy.

As not only our conscious mind but also our subconscious mind shifts to a higher state, our attitude will become one of willingness (level 310) and acceptance (level 350). We will no longer roll up and down with the random events of life. We are no longer fighting life, but have relaxed, released and let go. We will be in an almost continuous state of optimism that each event that surfaces in our life is perfectly calculated to expand our spiritual understanding and capacity for love and joy. This state of mind is not one that we force ourselves into, but rather that spontaneously and easily arises, maintained without any force or effort at all.

One of the signs that this change is truly occurring is the appearance of spiritual signs in our lives. When we speak things and they instantly or shortly manifest, then this is a sign that our minds are beginning to be aligned with our hearts. God knows what we want before we even ask it and provides these things in abundance. Effectively, this is a state where our every prayer of the heart, spoken or not, quickly comes into being.

Our natural state of being before we came into this mortal state was that of creators, children of the Most-High Creator. Creation through action we understand very well in this world. We go to work and make things happen with our own two hands. However, the ability to create with power is something less familiar to us.

Not only do we share the Most-High Creator's ability to create with our hands, but we also have his ability to create with our hearts. Not only do the Father and Christ respond to our prayers directly, but the light that is in all things and through all things, of which God is a fullness, responds to what is in our heart. The prayers of our heart are brought back to us, oftentimes before we even fully know what those prayers are.

This ability to have events happen through faith is often stifled by the subconscious clutter in our hearts. In other words, purify our hearts, and we will see signs manifest on their own. The righteous desires of our hearts will spontaneously come into being almost without any effort on our part. This is not due to us, but the Spirit that is in us.

A number of months ago, I had a dream in which I "woke up." I realized that I was in a dream. Knowing that I was in a dream filled me with joy. I saw and understood the connection between my emotional state or vibration and the contents that were being created in my dream. Not only could I create specific items or events in my dream, but I saw that the more joy I had, the better the dream got as a whole, even without my effort to create. The better the dream got, the more joy I had, which perpetuated the cycle.

I saw that there was a parallel between this understanding and life. What we put in our hearts comes back to us. If we desire fear because that is what is in our heart, then we shall receive our fears. If we desire joy and love, because that is what is in our hearts, then that will come back to us.

There is a difference between what is in our minds and what is in our hearts. Although we all carry desire in our minds for joy, what is in our hearts is often sending out the opposite message. As we learn to purify our hearts, then our lives become better. This is not always because we have changed the world so much that there is no more hardship or wrongdoing. But rather, because we have connected so fully with God's love and are in such a state of acceptance, that we allow him to use everything that shows up, the good and the bad, to bless us.

But even as we learn to use all things for our good, even as we learn to submit to God in all things, the day will come when we no longer need hardship to learn or heal. The day will come when we no longer need hardship for our brothers and sisters to learn either. We will all arrive at the fullness of the knowledge of God.

In the meantime, it can be helpful to see that we have been blind to our powers of creation even as an infant is unaware of whose hand it is that keeps hitting its face. The infant may desire the outside influence to stop, never being aware that it is his own hand. So too with our creations. We may be blind to them, but others on the other side of the veil are not. They are all too willing, both the light and the dark, to help us use this power of creation more effectively.

Like any skill, there are things we can do to improve our creation through faith. In previous chapters, we discussed purifying the subconscious. The interesting thing about purifying the heart is that often when we are done, the things we thought we wanted, we no longer desire. But to the extent that we still desire them, they will be granted. For all we put into our hearts with real intent, that is all we put into our hearts with real joy, even godly joy, and that we release the outcome unto God is brought back to us.

Godly joy is not the kind of joy we have here on earth. This is why we create so many negative things. It is part of our purpose here to have reflected back to us the desires of our hearts, both the positive and the negative. In this way, we can see and learn from both the pain and the joy. This process of learning is a type of joy before God. We may not always enjoy it, but the learning and progression of his children are joyful to him.

Therefore, to have the kind of joy that manifests is not always to be in a state of enjoyment. Rather, it is to acknowledge the higher or greater need. This does not mean that we cannot create things that seem frivolous. Sometimes the creations that manifest the fastest are the most frivolous.

My daughter and I were walking home from church one day. She was laughing and talking about one of my manifestations earlier in the week. I had been discussing brownies and how much I wanted some. As we pulled into our home, we found brownies on the doorstep.

As she reminded me of that experience, she said, "Dad, I want to do that again, but this time I want mint chocolate chip brownies!" I laughed with her. We were just joking around. And I told her I thought that was great, but what I wanted with it was the piece of property we were walking by at that moment with the creek on it.

Within an hour of getting home, there was a knock on our door. It was some of the neighbors we had yet to meet. They were holding mint chocolate chip brownies. It also turned out that they were the owners of that very piece of property I had been looking at!

Events like these can seem like coincidences, but when they show up repeatedly they cease to be coincidences and start to become creations. They become so many answered prayers from God.

My eight-year-old daughter seemed to be the best at this out of all of us. She was the most naturally joyful and trusting. Whenever we go places she manifests all kinds of candy and soda. She will simply say something like,

I really would like a soda, and then someone will walk over out of the blue and say they have an overwhelming desire to buy her one.

Again, creations through faith do not need to be serious in order to come into being. Sometimes, the more joy and child-like laughter that comes with them, the more likely they are to happen.

One day I was taking a shower and noticed I was out of shampoo. I decided I wanted to try sending a message to my wife. I dropped into my heart-center and felt her presence. In my mind's eye, I shook her on her shoulder, saying "I need you! I need you!" with a great deal of excitement and then ran off laughing like a teenage prankster. Needless to say, I had a great deal of mirth in this regardless of the outcome.

A few minutes later, my wife walked into the bathroom and said, "Honey, do you need something? The Holy Ghost just told me that you needed me." I burst out laughing and told her what I had done. She stormed off angry, telling me that it was inappropriate for me to use Spirit for such trivial things, all of which set me off laughing even harder. While I ended up having to get my own shampoo, I learned something and got a laugh at the same time.

These spiritual creations are not limited to brownies or property or shampoo. The types of things that can be created with faith are innumerable. They can include other things that seem miraculous, like the development of spiritual gifts, teachings from heaven, a better job and almost anything imaginable.

The process for creation through faith is relatively simple. As with other faith-based intentions, there really isn't a right or wrong way to go about it. All techniques are used to get you to a place where you can exercise the faith and let go but are not the action of letting go itself.

Aspects of faith-based creation that I have found helpful include: 1) Move into your center or connect with God in your preferred way 2) Envision and especially feel what it is that you want. 3) Let go of the outcome, trusting that whatever happens God is in control and it will be perfect for your growth and highest joy.

Connecting with God can help us bring the maximum amount of light into our creation. It also helps us to release negative emotions like fear or doubt. This connection allows us to be more present with the part of us that actually has resonance with God's light and can make our conscious mind more congruent with our hearts. While dropping into heart space is one way to establish this connection, other methods might include spending time relaxing in a spiritual or holy place or doing a meditation or prayer that uses visuals and feelings of moving into God's presence or light.

Envisioning is more than imagination. It is a state of mind where you let go and allow things to show up in your mind. It is like taking the markers from the mind's whiteboard and giving them to God and angels to play with. In this way, what is really in your heart is *revealed* not imagined. Revelation in this process can help unify the heart and the mind.

While envisioning, you want to engage as many of the senses as possible, especially the *feelings*. We often think that a new job or more money will make us happy, but what we really want is not the thing itself. What we really want is the feeling we think the thing will give us. Having a deep level of honesty in our creations will help us be more in tune with heaven. It is not that manifesting money is bad, just that for most of us, it is not what we really want. What we really want is the feeling of safety, security, value or happiness. When we connect with these emotions, we can be more honest with heaven about what it is we truly want and then give heaven greater flexibility to respond.

In my experience, what I think I want is not usually granted until I have uncovered what it is I truly want. Then, I am more prepared to receive the requests of my heart. This process can be slow or painful, especially if we are not used to being honest with ourselves about what it is we really want.

This process of identifying what we truly want is therapeutic. It can allow us to release a lot of societal or family beliefs that are no longer useful in our journey to God. Thus, even the truly trivial creations are used by heaven to teach us and to heal us. There are no trivial creations before God. There is nothing little or unimportant. It all has a purpose. The highest of all those purposes is joy and enlightenment (look back at the chart and notice where these rank on the scale of emotions).

As it turns out, the most powerful emotions connected with creation are those of love, peace, and joy. These emotions when authentically connected with our faith-based creations seem to produce the greatest results. If these are not the emotions behind your creation, you may want to consider why it is you truly want what it is you are trying to create through faith.

If you see something you don't want while you are envisioning, or emotions come up that are not part of what you want to create, step back, reconnect with God and try again. Continue to envision until you get it right. There are no limits on how many times you can try.

Be specific in what you are envisioning. Sometimes the specifics are fun because they seem to confirm the creation. In one of my manifestations, I decided that I wanted the company I worked for to settle some outstanding debts. I described how I wanted this to be done. There was always involvement of lawyers as a possibility, but I did not want to receive the money that way.

I specified that I wanted a new investor to come into the picture that asked the company to deal with my debt. I wanted the company to come to me and for it to be a favor to them for me to resolve that debt with them. This was the exact opposite feeling of getting a lawyer involved. I envisioned the words that were said. I specified how much I wanted up front and how much I wanted on an ongoing basis.

Within a month or so of that manifestation, I received a phone call from my company. The company was bringing in a new investor and they needed to resolve my debt. When I came in to meet with the board, the first numbers they proposed to me were the very ones I had written down for my manifestation. Again, I could call it coincidence, but it all worked out according to my joy.

The third step is equally if not more critical than the step of envisioning what you want. Letting go is where the power is. Letting go is not pretending to be ok with the outcome no matter what. It is actually being in a place where you know you will have just as much joy and growth from God without what you are asking for as with it. It arises spontaneously and effort free from the heart. It is a sincere feeling. This does not come by destroying your joy in what you are asking for, but by increasing your joy and your hope in the present moment and your overall faith and trust in God.

We can let go in the moment by moving into our heart center, to that space of no thought or emotion. But as often happens, we come back out of that state and we are confronted with reality. Depending on what we are creating, we may have hidden hurts about the particular subject matter. If we do, you are going to see those hurts and fears surface and heal before you see what you are manifesting.

I do not wish to create a limitation by making that statement, but it has happened every time for me. If there is healing to be done, then I get the chance to do some of that healing before I see the manifestation come to fruition. Those hurts and fears are often times the very blocks that need to be resolved in order for faith to be exercised, or in order to be in a place of true and sincere acceptance.

If you find that there are blocks to your creations, then dig deep to understand the hurts and the fears. If there are walls up or rigidity of any sort, you can move back into your center to let them go. As these clear and as God heals them, you will be in a place to manifest what you are seeking if you still desire it. Oftentimes in healing the hurts, what we want changes. When we are healed, we no longer desire what we once thought was important.

If what you are manifesting does not seem to materialize, but the opposite materializes, maintain a positive outlook. Letting go does not mean that you are perfectly happy in every moment while waiting for the creation to come back to you, but it does mean that you stay in your highest joy. I have found that even if I am hurting deeply, if I will ask what I would be doing in the moment if I were in my highest joy, I will see something come into my mind. By staying in the flow of what my joy would be if I could have joy, my manifestations still seem to come to fruition.

The other trick is to stay focused on what you want, not on what you don't want. Similar to looking at where you want to be on the road rather than the pothole that you don't want to hit, where you put your attention is generally where you go. Again, this is easier if you are in a space of neutrality where you have truly let go. Then it is not a matter of clinging as a way of covering up the fears we are subconsciously creating instead of what we want, but our hearts spontaneously produce the focus.

To build your faith, let go of the blocks that tell you that you cannot create with faith. Let go of the rigidity that is inside of you. Open to new possibilities. Keep a log book of your efforts, and especially write the results down as they come. This can help you recognize those miracles that come rather than discounting them as coincidences. The more of these "coincidences" you have in your logbook, the harder it will be to not accept them as true evidence of your faith.

Start small. As your faith builds, create larger things. Make it a game. When you take the seriousness out of it, it can be more fun and more fun usually works better. You can also work with a partner. Have them visualize it with you.

Sometimes voicing what you are seeing or writing it down can make it more real. When you are working with a partner or a group, if you see something show up in Spirit and they see it too, it can act as a second witness to really strengthen your faith.

If you are not seeing or feeling much, start with what you do feel or see. If you cannot imagine how the event or item you are trying to create can be done, start with the feeling. Remember that faith is about a *feeling* more than it is about *seeing*. To have faith is not to see the end from the beginning. You simply know the feeling that you are seeking and let God fill in the details.

As with the dream I related earlier, it is not necessary to specify everything you want to show up in your life. Sometimes it can be more fun and exercise greater faith to simply let go and trust in God to bring back your highest joy and growth. Remember that our highest joy is not always fun. Sometimes it involves deeply riveting healing experiences. But if we can let go and trust God, then even these can be joyful in their own way.

For your consideration:

- What are some of the creations you have been praying for that haven't materialized the way you wanted? Close your eyes, relax and ask what the worst thing would be about getting what you've been asking for? Or alternatively, ask what the best thing is about not getting what you are asking for? Follow the digging process to the root.
- Try a faith-based creation using visuals and emotion. Pray to God like you normally would, but then drop into your heart and open yourself

to what it is that you truly want. Allow yourself to visualize it in every detail. Especially feel the joy of the emotion that comes from receiving what you are visualizing. Thank God that you already have it and let it go.

- Write down what you manifest. It will surprise you how many of these types of prayers are answered and with what degree of specificity, some immediately and some a year or more later. Writing them down will help you remember that you asked for these and you will recognize how many have been answered in time. This will increase your faith and your ability to have even greater manifestations.

CHAPTER

11

The Role of Faith in the World's Transition

One of the signs of faith transition in the subconscious has to do with our faith in the end times. When Jonah was sent to preach to Nineveh, he did it with a form of spiritual pride. His value was in his righteousness. Because he was righteous he would be preserved, while those in Nineveh should be destroyed because of the prophecy of God. He was severely disappointed when Nineveh was not destroyed based on the word of God.

So what happened with Jonah? Was he not a prophet because his prophecy failed? Were his words not valid? Did God lie? How did the future change from that which was written?

Our problem is that we often look at the future like it is fixed. This is a very Calvinistic viewpoint that denies agency. The future is variable. When the word of God is given, it describes the most likely future to happen based on the *present* actions of society.

The future looks less like a single continuous thread and more like the unwound tip of a piece of rope with many strands coming off of it. There are many different possible futures branching off from the present. The one thread immediately in front of us, assuming nothing changes, is the god-thread. This is the thread described in prophecy. It is not the only path, but it is the path that will occur if nothing changes.

Some prophecies are given as signs so that we can recognize a true prophet. Their fulfillment does not depend on the agency of those listening. However, most prophecies are directed at the agency of the listeners. They are not given so that they will happen, but so that we can learn from the god-thread before it happens. This is the type of prophecy that Jonah gave. It was not a prophecy to prove his prophetic stature, but to warn the people so they could change before the god-thread came into being. Jonah's prophecy was never meant to happen, *but to be overcome through faith.*

When we exercise faith in the destruction of the world according to prophecy, that is not faith at all, but a form of spiritual pride similar to what Jonah experienced. Rather than exercising faith that the world can change and be spared, we are contributing to the forces that will actually destroy the world. What would have happened if the people of Nineveh simply accepted the prophecy of Jonah as the "unchangeable" will of God? What would have happened if they said, "Oh well, better get our food storage?"

When we think of the end of the world, perhaps some of us hold the belief that the end could change if the people in the world around us repented, but we have no faith in their willingness or ability to do so. What is interesting about this viewpoint is that our agency becomes subject to other people's use of their agency. We become victims as it were to their choices. But as we release the stuck places inside of us, especially fear, guilt and shame, we begin to find that we are never victims. We are powerful creators, and God responds to all the true desires of our hearts.

The belief that the world's destruction is linked to the unwillingness of others to change is similar to the point of view Jonah held. He had no faith in Nineveh's ability or willingness to change. He could not see how their potential destruction rested more with his own unbelief than in theirs. But even the small change in faith in Jonah's heart to go and deliver the prophecy was enough to reverse the very god-thread he just preached. Just the addition of the smoldering ember of faith of a single reluctant person changed what would have happened. It was not a change in the faith of the people of Nineveh that prevented the destruction of Nineveh so much as it was the tiniest of changes in the faith in the heart of Jonah, the one person to whom God actually spoke. This mustard seed of faith in the heart of one person changed everything.

Although it may be hard to believe that one person can affect the god-thread so powerfully, yet all it takes is one measure of leavening to leaven the whole. It is not the fault of the flour when the bread does not rise, but that of the leavening. It is the leavening who must lift with faith in order for the world to be preserved, and it is the hope and faith of those that are called leavening that causes us to rise.

When we consider that we are the creators of what happens in this world through the beliefs we hold in our heart, then the finger of blame pointed outwards starts to turn inwards. Reflect for a moment on the answer to this question, what group of people holds the strongest beliefs in the destruction of the world? Which group of people looks for that destruction night and day? Although we believe it is the iniquity of the world that will bring destruction upon it, what group of people is most asking for this destruction by the beliefs in their hearts? So who is it that most has the opportunity to change what happens in the world through a change in the faith they are exercising? Was the book of Revelation written to the non-believers or the Christians? Who was it a warning to? Who is it that actually has the power to change that god-thread through the exercise of a greater form of faith? Who is the leavening called to leaven the whole?

It is interesting to note that the prophecies of destruction as given by Isaiah and even by John are directed first towards God's own people. Why? Because they are the leavening to leaven the whole. They must be first purified because they are the ones who first need to have faith to prepare the way for the rest of the world. The real repentance that needs to take place is not so much in the world around us but in the hearts of God's own people. We are the ones who are falling short in faith that the world can change, that God is that great. We are the ones who are stuck in judgment and the demands for justice through the end of the world.

When James and John asked to bring fire down on a village that rejected Jesus, Jesus responded that they did not know what manner of God that they served. If this is true of a village, then how much more true of a world that rejects him? Jesus came not to condemn the world or to destroy people's lives, but to save them. It is our role and privilege as his disciples to let go of our own guilt, shame, and fears of judgment that we unconsciously project on the world around us and to start to exercise faith in something better. It is for the leavening to have the hope of change and the possibility of a peaceful transition for the world. If we do not have that hope, then who will?

Since we are children of the Most-High Creator and since we do create through our hearts, what if we stopped powering destruction with our faith and put our faith in something better? What if we let go of the fear programs that are locking us into the creation of destruction and started to exercise hope in a more peaceful transition into the new world? How many people would it take exercising faith in something better for the world to change? How many people did God tell Abraham it would take to spare Sodom and Gomorrah? And wasn't it just Abraham, a single individual, who secured that promise? Are we not told that it was through faith that the Law of Moses was given, but that it was also through faith that something better was granted?

What if instead of fear and spiritual pride, we planted hope in our hearts? What if we planted the possibility of change? What if we planted the pure love of Jesus Christ? Do we understand how our faith literally changes the world? Do we understand that end-time prophecies, including those seen in near-death experiences, were not given so they would happen, but so that they could be overcome? This is the ultimate test of faith for God's people. Will they simply capitulate their faith because of the impossibility of the task, or will they actually have enough faith to ask with real intent for something better?

This is not to say that we should not be wise servants. Prepare by the Spirit in peace, love, hope, and joy. Simply go not out with haste or with fear, but prepare in love. Trust in God who leads us, all the while exercising faith in something better. Use the power of faith-based creation within you to open a new path to heaven on earth.

Let it not be said of Zion because of the lack of faith of her Christian sons and daughters, "There is none to guide her among all the sons whom she hath brought forth; neither is there any that taketh her by the hand of all the sons that she hath brought up." (Isa 51:18) Rather, let us heed the prophetic warning, "Awake, awake, put on strength, O arm of the Lord; awake, as in the ancient days, in the generations of old. Art thou not it that hath cut Rahab, and wounded the dragon? Art thou not it which hath dried the sea, the waters of the great deep; that hath made the depths of the sea a way for the ransomed to pass over?" (Isa 51:9-10) Truly, when we take back our power of faith-based creation and start to use it to not only produce miracles but to impact the god-thread, we will be the leavening that the Lord's people were always meant to be.

For your consideration:

- What blocks do you have, if any, about the world transitioning in a more peaceful way? Using stream of consciousness or another form of clearing, close your eyes, relax and ask what would be the worst thing if the world transitioned without any conflict? Remember to confront the emotion head on. With whatever answer comes up, ask what the worst thing would be about that. Keep digging until you find the root.

- Now try the flip side of the exercise. Ask, what would be the best thing if the world transitioned without any conflict? If you need to, ask as many times as necessary, "But what if it were possible, what would be the best thing?" Whatever answer you get, ask what the best thing would be about that? Keep going until you feel the emotion shift.
- Have a conversation with God. Is it even possible for the world to transition differently than spoken of in scriptures? Ask if the answer you are receiving could change if the beliefs in your heart changed? How many people need to have this type of faith for it to change? Who needs to have this type of faith for it to change?
- Try an envisioning exercise for a faith-based creation. Do it with a like-minded partner if possible. Drop deep into your heart space and connect with the light. What do you see, feel, hear or otherwise notice about the end time transition? Allow Spirit to surprise you with what is possible. Remember that the prayer of the heart, especially as led by Spirit can have a tremendous impact. As you do this exercise, how do you feel exercising faith and hope for something better?

CHAPTER

12

Application and Ascension

The world is transitioning. There are elements of every major religion that recognize this. Even non-religious people among the new age community are receiving daily direction about the transition that is coming. Truly, light and knowledge are being poured out over the entire world; well might an individual stretch forth their puny arm to turn the Missouri River from its decreed course as to stop the Almighty from pouring out light and knowledge on his children around the world.

Using the metaphor of Paul describing the different types of glories that exist in the resurrection, we can understand the coming changes upon the earth. "There is one glory of the sun, and another glory of the moon, and another glory of the stars: for one star differeth from another star in glory." (I Cor 15:41) This metaphor implies that there is a difference in joy in the heavens as great as the difference in the light we see from the stars, moon, and sun. Currently, we could say that the earth and those who reside upon it reside in the lowest glory or in the state with the lowest potential for joy which is comparable to the light we see from the stars.

The coming changes will take the earth and its highest form of understanding from that of a glory similar to the stars to a glory similar to that of the moon. Scientifically, that is a 10,000 fold increase in light. This means that even the best understandings of God will be as handcarts compared to the knowledge that is brought forth in the coming days and years. Even then, the earth will go through another transition that takes it from the glory of the moon to that of the sun, scientifically a 400,000 fold increase in light, understanding, and joy. As it has been said, God's ways are truly above our ways, as the heavens are above the earth.

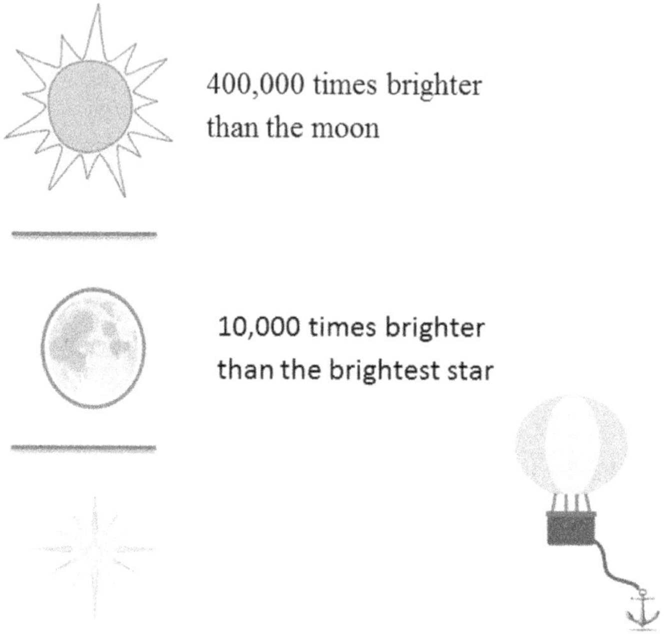

Ascension is the process of comprehending and replacing lower vibration emotions and beliefs with higher vibration ones, similar to how a hot air balloon rises.

Figure 4

The vibration of the earth and its people will be raised to be able to handle the vibration of the presence of our God. God's energy is brighter and hotter than the sun. Shortly after the Big Bang, the heat and energy given off were so intense that not even the subatomic particles that make up the atoms in the sun could exist. In other words, God experiences a joy so intense that his presence would be capable of melting the sun, and any who hope to remain on earth in his presence must be changed. Ascension, which is the physical and spiritual process to be prepared to abide and enjoy the vibration of God, is being taught in one form or another among all of God's children. Despite their differences, each path has elements of 1) belief in some form of spiritual progression 2) a way to either passively or actively clear low vibration understanding and replace it with higher understanding 3) inner guidance.

Among ascension groups that I have visited with, studied among or heard about, many spiritual gifts are being taught openly to those who have the dedication and perseverance to reach the highest levels of study. These gifts include healing, creation through faith, opening portals in time and space, changing the properties of matter, and changing the properties of the physical body among others. These gifts are acquired independent of religious background and require only a pure heart and mind to operate (eg they have released lower vibration beliefs and emotions in favor of higher vibration ones). Remember that those who abide in the earth's higher states will be of many religions, including non-Christians. The changes in the body necessary for this and the gifts available will be poured out upon all peoples, although some may find a more particular kind of joy in their association with Christ.

These diverse spiritual gifts will be brought into the New Jerusalem to crown, glorify and exalt her. These are the gifts that ancient prophets saw bestowed upon the Holy City by the gentiles. It is the gathering of the spiritual gifts and knowledge into one whole that will raise and glorify God's people. Then with the crown of understanding complete, the crowning jewel of the testimony of Jesus Christ and his role can be added for the glory of all.

Creating Zion, the Pure in Heart

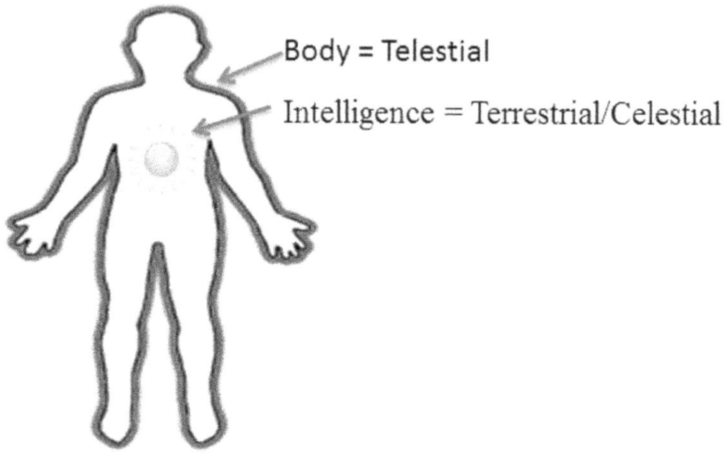

The piece of god light that God placed within us in the beginning contains a perfect replica of all the light in Him. Thus, we were created in His image with all of His potential.

Identifying with the body as separate from God is a telestial state. Feeling our connection with God through the light is part of our terrestrial/celestial state.

Figure 5

We understand that there is a light that is in all things and through all things. This light has been called by many names, including the Light of Truth, the Light of Christ and even Intelligence. Father is the physical expression of a fullness of this Light and Intelligence that is in all things and through all things. Jesus Christ progressed to become like Father by becoming a fullness of this Light.

Each of God's creations has this light within them. It is the Intelligence that gives them the ability to act and not be acted upon. Thus, all creation is made out of this god-light. They cannot exist otherwise. Therefore, we are never separate from God, we only appear to be in the illusion of this world.

Buddhists and Hindus have long understood this concept. Their ultimate goal of a conscious awareness of enlightened unity with a fullness of this god-light is really the first step towards unity in a millennial reign. What Buddhists and Hindus do not generally understand is that while enlightened unity with god-light by oneself is 10,000 times more glorious (the glory of the moon compared to the stars) than anything we know in this world, experiencing that in the physical presence of our Father God is 400,000 times more glorious still (the glory of the sun compared to the moon). With the foundation of the eastern view of enlightenment paving the way into a terrestrial state, it is the crowning truth of Christ that lifts the world still higher into the physical presence of God. Once again, it is the combination of the key or essential truths of each perspective that give us a more complete picture of the whole.

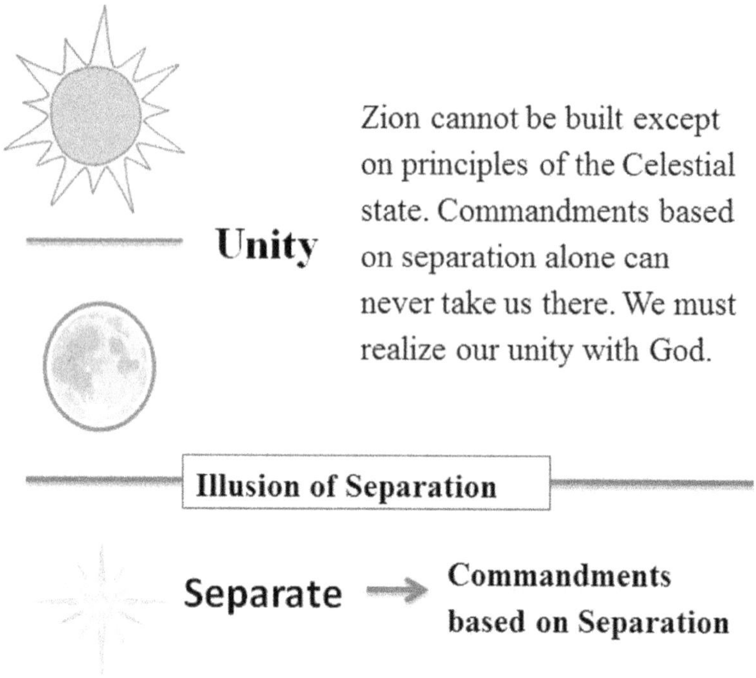
Unity
Zion cannot be built except on principles of the Celestial state. Commandments based on separation alone can never take us there. We must realize our unity with God.
Illusion of Separation
Separate
Commandments based on Separation

Figure 6

Due to the appearance of separation in this world, we feel lack and hurt among other things. Commandments were given to prevent lack and hurt in this state of separation. We sometimes assume these commandments were designed to return us to a Celestial state, but they are a reaction to the illusion of separation. Overreliance on the law alone without an understanding of redemption and grace can reinforce the illusion of separation, creating the opposite effect of what we were intending.

This may be why God through Isaiah condemned His covenant people for *living* the law given to them, comparing them with Sodom and Gomorrah (see Isa 1:10-14). Their belief in salvation by obedience to the law alone blinded them to the true purpose of the law in pointing their souls to Christ and to liberation from the law. The law was starting to harden their hearts to the light rather than to change their hearts through faith in the Messiah. In fact, it was their blindness to the light due to their rigid obedience to the letter of the law without any regard for its purpose that led them to crucify Christ and martyr his apostles hundreds of years later.

The difference between Christ's disciples and those that martyred him was not their obedience, for they were all obedient. In fact, if anything, those who martyred Christ were more obedient to the letter of the law as understood in their day. Rather the difference was in Christ's disciples receiving the Spirit that consecrated the path of their obedience under the law unto salvation. They used the law to increase their light rather than to diminish it like those men who crucified Christ. Obedience to the law without the Spirit is death; while obedience to the law in Spirit is life; "for the letter killeth, but the spirit giveth life." (2 Cor 3:6)

It is the same in our day; the five wise virgins who abide the day of his coming by virtue of having oil in their lamps have taken the Spirit to be their guide, while the five virgins who are cast out did not. If we understand that Isaiah used a form of doublespeak in not only speaking to God's ancient covenant people but more especially to His covenant people today preceding the return of Jesus Christ, then we understand that we are in danger of falling into the same trap as ancient Israel.

Salvation is not in the law alone; it serves only as a reminder of deeper truths that must be taken into our hearts. It is the deeper truths that the law points to that save. For the truth shall set you free. If not so, then how are they that knew no law in this life saved? How are the infants or the mentally handicapped saved? The law is the schoolmaster and governs all of its own, but salvation is of grace.

While adherence to the telestial commandments can give us the best of experiences in this world where we have the appearance of separation from God, obedience to them alone cannot return us to the Celestial state. The training wheels help us to learn to ride the bicycle, but they are not the bicycle itself.

The law of Zion and of the Celestial state is unity in the pure love of God; Zion is the pure in heart, those of one heart and one mind. Zion is the place where none needs instruct their brother to know God, for all know him, from the least to the greatest. This is the new covenant that God promised to make with his people. (Heb 8:8-13)

In addition to protecting us in this telestial state, the telestial commandments serve to teach us contrast by showing us that we can never be redeemed by the law, that we never have to earn God's love or salvation, *because we never were separate from it to begin with.* Redemption comes through the revelation of Jesus Christ and through grace, which releases our hearts and our minds from the powerful illusion of separation from God.

In order to transition from a telestial to a terrestrial state, we must let go of our lower vibration beliefs that we earn salvation, and allow the grace of Jesus Christ to restore us to the knowledge that we can never be separate from God. In other words, we cease to identify as the body which appears separate, and we begin to identify with the light that is in all things and through all things. This process cannot be forced or earned, it can only be manifested and allowed.

We understand that Zion can only be established on principles of the *Celestial* kingdom in a state of unity. Therefore, we can only go so far in the establishment of Zion on principles of the telestial law based on separation. We must awaken to our true state of connectedness with God. We must awaken to the light within and remember our connection to all things.

Remembering Wholeness

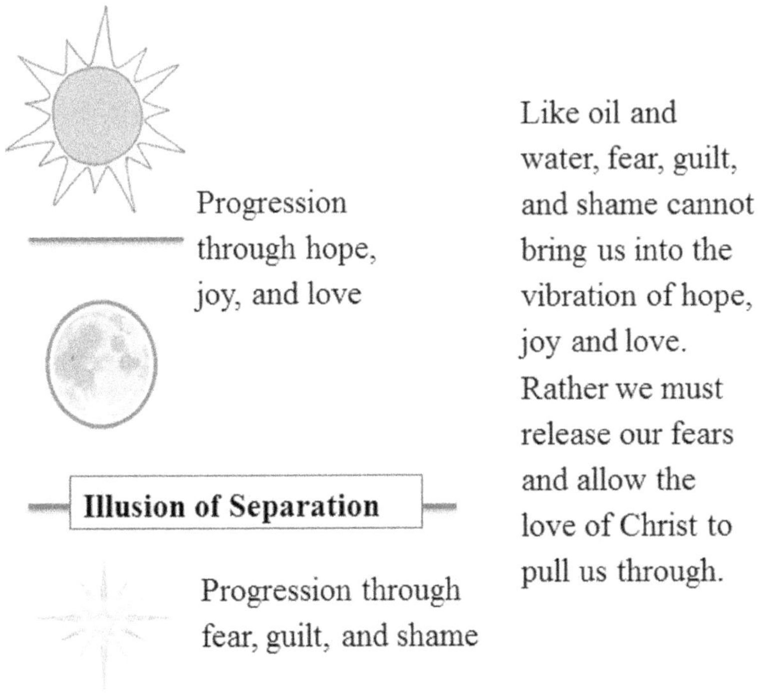

Progression through hope, joy, and love
Illusion of Separation
Progression through fear, guilt, and shame
Like oil and water, fear, guilt, and shame cannot bring us into the vibration of hope, joy and love. Rather we must release our fears and allow the love of Christ to pull us through.

Figure 7

This remembering of our true identities and connection with God will give us the joy of the higher vibration state while we are going through the additional changes in belief structure necessary to create higher vibration bodies and experiences. It is important to understand that while in the fallen world we are compelled to ascend through fear, guilt, and shame, in the higher state, we can only ascend through experiencing and feeling authentic love and joy. Thus, remembering wholeness will actually increase the rate at which we are able to ascend.

The most important step to remembering wholeness is taking the Spirit to be your guide. It is through the Spirit that you will be guided in how to make all of your transition. Although we may be taught by enlightened individuals, angels or even resurrected beings, our direct connection with God must always be how we learn from these different sources. It is through the Spirit that we receive what God wants us to know free from the filters and limitations of others.

The growth itself happens through the mechanism of God's grace. By definition, there is nothing that you can do to earn grace. You can only allow it. This means that your fastest path of growth will be the one in which you walk your joy, whatever that may be. It is in loving yourself truly and fully, which will cause you to walk the path of your joy, that you will be most open to allowing God's grace. It is on this path that your ascension will move at its proper rate. Whatever that looks like, no matter how fast or slow, it will be important to love yourself and the plan that you chose with God before this life.

Opening and allowing the grace of Christ into our lives is most effectively achieved by individuals who love themselves enough that they are able to be present and find joy in each moment. There is an understanding that the flesh is not mere illusion as depicted in the eastern philosophies or temptation as believed in the western religions, but a loving gift from God for our experience and ultimate exaltation.

As Christians, we frequently open to the Spirit illuminating our bodies, but we misunderstand the purpose of the flesh that clothes the light within us. We fight against it. We hate it. We despise it for the hurt we have felt and call it sinful and evil.

Spirit and the elements which clothe our spirits inseparably connected receive a fullness of joy. This is after the pattern of our Heavenly Parents. The matter that our spirits now occupy is still only partially organized. It has not yet arrived at the stature of the bodies of our Heavenly Parents. By entering into these mortal tabernacles, we undertake the effort to further organize the matter that comprises them. We experience its fallen state and God through us raises it still higher.

It is this purification process of matter that we see with the release of lower vibration beliefs and emotions. These lower vibration thought forms and emotions are the byproducts or potentially even the cause of partially organized matter. As we release these beliefs and emotions and replace them with higher vibration thoughts and emotions, we continue the ascension of our mortal bodies and all other matter in this earth plane.

Just as the light within us is connected to all things and through all things, so too are our lower vibration thoughts and emotions part of the matrix of unbelief that makes up the veil of our fallen world. As we overcome the unbelief within our own bodies and raise them, we contribute to the lifting of the entire world in preparation for the return of Jesus Christ. It will be in this higher vibration state of openness and unity that we will finally be capable of receiving the revelation of joy that he is bringing. Our purification process is still not complete.

Instead of despising our bodies and our life situations, instead of viewing them as sinful or evil as thought in many western religions, or as an illusion as believed in eastern philosophies, we embrace them as gifts. We love them the way we might love a mistreated and misunderstood child. Or even as the love of a good man has the power to lift and change a woman with low self-esteem in ways that bring eternal fruits, so too does our love and presence have the power to change our bodies.

In a marriage between a man and a woman, the man is a symbol of the light or Intelligence while the woman is a symbol of the mortal tabernacle filled by this light. When we allow the light, or the masculine, to love and appreciate the mortal tabernacle, or the feminine, by entering fully into her rather than cutting off from her and despising her, the power of creation is unlocked. Embracing our mortal states, not rejecting them, is the path forward to allowing the carnal/natural person to become a saint through the atonement of Christ.

The indigenous populations of the world possess some of the few traditions in this world that revere the sacred nature of creation in such a way. They understand the importance of their earth 'Mother' and love her. They see their time in this physical world as a gift. It is not something to be fought against or controlled, but rather loved and respected. This love and respect do not take away from the importance of the spiritual 'Father' energy, but it recognizes that God's purposes are not fulfilled without the blessing of matter and our brief sojourn in these mortal bodies.

We must understand that the matter that clothes us is as the loving touch of a woman and is faithful to us to a fault. It responds to the requests of the light or Intelligence within us with perfect obedience, bringing back to us all experience that we require. Nothing that appears in our lives is by accident. It is all by divine design. How can we hate that matter which clothes us with so much love and which serves us unfailingly and unceasingly in our need to have experience for our exaltation?

Thus, to love one's self, we must also love the bodies we have been given including their emotional and mental states. It is all a gift for which we can be grateful. This kind of self-love is not ego or pride. In fact, pride is the opposite of self-love. It is an avoidance of the pain that comes from a lack of self-love. Self-love is the key that opens the door to feeling God's love for us continuously. It is one of the virtues that makes God independently joyful, and if we are to become like him, then we must learn to develop it as he has.

There is pain and there is joy in this path. But in all things, it is important to plant the belief that no matter what happens it will inure to your greatest joy. This is because you are creating your reality. Without faith, nothing happens. Or rather, without this faith, you will create the default, subconscious programs planted within your carnal/natural person.

Effects of Identifying with the Light within

There are a number of immediate and longer-term changes that are brought about to the degree that we become aware that we are the light within. The first and most important of these has to do with our connection to God. We realize that we were never separate from him and can never be separate from his love. This means we no longer need to teach our neighbor to know God, for all in this state know him from the least to the greatest. Each has that intimate connection within them that is far closer than being in his physical presence and can access a full knowledge of God and his plans for them at the rate that brings them their highest joy.

In this state of connectedness, we begin to love ourselves the way that God loves himself. God is joyfully stable no matter what those around him may choose. As we learn to love ourselves the way that God loves himself, our joyful vibration becomes stable and constant. Nothing can take it away.

In this state of connectedness and fullness of joy, there is no more lack and no possibility to create harm for one another. Those laws that were based on the assumption of separation from God cease to exist or are changed at the rate that individuals wake up to their wholeness. Rather than entering heaven from an infinite confinement of increasing law, they are made free to an infinite degree to follow their joy and bring glory to God. This process does not happen through the abolition of the law, but rather the comprehension and replacement of lower vibration law with higher vibration law.

For example, Jesus's ability to walk on water does not come through the abolition of the law of gravity, but rather through the raising of his consciousness to a state in which higher laws apply. God is not an inmate to the laws of the telestial state, and to the degree that we release our limited understanding and become like God, those same changes may be enacted in us.

It is also important to note that although we may be consciously aware of all these changes that are coming and may even have a witness of them from Spirit, until our subconscious has been freed from low vibration law, we should continue to act in the way we have been taught. Even though Father does not judge us, we unconsciously judge ourselves by the law implanted in our subconscious which both creates and returns to us the consequences of our own self-judgment. Therefore, we should follow the Spirit in allowing these changes to unfold in us naturally through the grace of Christ.

With an understanding of who we really are at our center, we begin to create through faith. We no longer need authority from another to act in our divine nature and potential. We recognize that each of us has god within us. As we truly understand that and act within it, our power to move, act and create in every situation increases. All that we joyfully put into our heart comes into being.

For your consideration:

- Reflect for a moment on why you are pursuing the faith to work miracles. Is there a deeper, divine purpose behind this?
- Have a conversation with God about the light within you. Who are you really? What does it mean that you are made in his image? What is your role in the ascension of the earth? What are the major blocks preventing you from consciously being who and what you really are?
- Reflect on your feelings, especially those deeply buried feelings, about your body and about being in this world. Are they positive or negative? Why?

You might use subconscious streaming to help you get out your real feelings and to release anything negative in connection with your sojourn in this body or in this world.

CHAPTER

13

Inner Guidance

In our journey back to God, in our journey to learn a deeper, more powerful faith, in our journey of ascension, there is one element we all will need to develop: faith in our inner guidance.

I am a convert to Christianity. As such, there are some basic understandings that I have been given that others born in the faith may not fully appreciate. When I made the decision to be baptized at age twenty one, it was not because my parents told me to, it was not because the Bible said to, it was not because my religious teachers told me to, it was because of the inner voice I heard that spoke to me. I was baptized because of Jesus Christ.

When I grew up, I did not grow up in a religious home. Although many people take for granted that the Bible is the word of God, it is the same in other cultures for other religious texts. When you grow up in a culture where there is no mention of God, then there are no religious texts which are authoritative and absolute. In that kind of a culture, no one acts because the Bible tells you to.

No one takes the authority of a religious teacher of the Bible as legitimate any more than they would a bunch of old wives' tales. So what is it that ultimately causes a person from a non-Christian background to convert to Christianity? It is the voice of Christ.

Saul of Tarsus was on the road to arrest and persecute Christians when Jesus appeared to him. He did not convert because of the authority of Jewish scripture. He did not convert because of the testimony of authoritative witnesses who had seen Christ after the resurrection. He converted because of the witness of Jesus to his own soul.

While the conversion of Saul, later known as Paul, could be considered dramatic, it is no less so for any person who makes the choice to become a disciple of Christ coming from a non-Christian culture. These people are often ostracized and shunned for their choices. In extreme cases, threats may be made against their lives by their own family members, the people to whom they should be able to look to for love and trust.

Any person coming from such a culture will understand that the divine authority rests first in our own internal witness. Divine authority rests with the witness of the Spirit of God within us and then in other sources that have been given to us to assist us.

Just as connecting to this internal guidance is essential for those who make the choice to become Christian, so too is it essential for all of those born in the Christian culture. Just because there is acceptance from birth of divine revelation contained in scripture or of individuals who teach that revelation, does not mean that the inner voice is no longer necessary. In fact for these people, the inner voice may be even more necessary. For it will lead them to understand all things they need to know to return to the presence of God.

There is no other person who stands between us and God. We understand that Jesus is the one who is our mediator. He employs no servant there and he cannot be deceived. All too often though, we trust his servants over the voice he has placed within us. Like the children of Israel when Moses went up the mount to converse with God, we would rather that others tell us what to do than come into the presence of God ourselves. In this way, we release ourselves from personal accountability. We make the trip easier.

The problem with this is that even if our religious leaders are perfectly inspired of God, we still need to receive their teachings through the Spirit in order for them to be of God. Our minds rely on the literal interpretation of the words and the immediate application of those words. Because each of us are individuals in different places, at times those words can be the exact opposite of what we need in the moment.

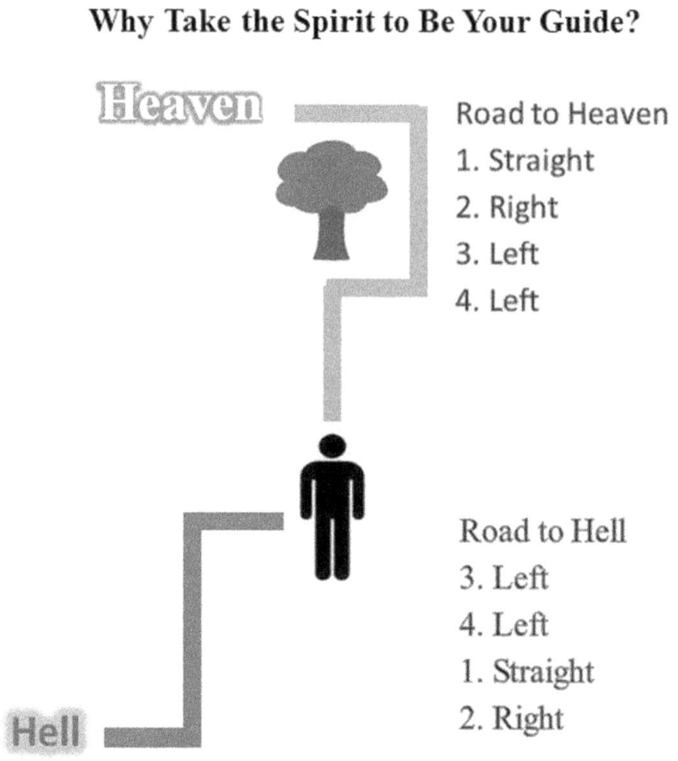

Even true instructions at the wrong time can lead you to unexpected places

Figure 8

The graphic above is overly simplistic and exploits the heaven/hell polarization, but illustrates a valid point. True instructions given in the wrong order can lead to an entirely different destination. Therefore, even if we assume our leaders are teaching the truth, we need to have the Spirit to know which instructions to apply when.

For example, I spent some time in Brazil as a missionary. Our religious leaders spoke to a large group of missionaries who I was with and suggested that we try to contact at least fifty people a week to talk about the gospel. I was already teaching such a large number of people before this suggestion that when I tried to follow their suggestion, we no longer had time to teach all the people who wanted to be baptized.

The following week, I consulted with my religious leader on the subject. He said, "When I said those things, I wasn't necessarily talking to you." He was expecting me to use the Spirit in applying his counsel, including if that meant doing the exact opposite of what was said. While talking to fifty people a week was definitely an inspired suggestion for the majority of missionaries in our area and even for me at other points in my missionary service, at that moment it was the wrong suggestion at the wrong time for me and the work that God had me doing.

The difference between the five wise virgins and the five foolish virgins in the parable of Christ was that the wise virgins brought their own light with them. They took the Holy Ghost to be their guide when the others simply tried to rely on the words and faith of others to get them there.

Although in our ascension process, we release fear-based motivation, there is still validity in the teaching from the figure. If you are unwilling to trust the guidance you receive directly from God, then God will place authority figures in your life who lead you astray. Then you will learn to trust your own divine authority. It will lead you to which scriptures to study when, where to look for other truths that are not as obvious in scripture, which teachers to listen to and when.

Over time, you will see a pattern. When you follow the internal guidance you will find rich rewards of understanding, truth, and edification. When you fail to listen to that internal guidance, then even teachers or scriptures that you have looked to in the past will become a trap to you.

Bear in mind that both beings of light and beings of dark know how to use the truth in scripture to affect you. When we listen to Spirit, we choose to let the beings of light give us the higher interpretations and applications of what is taught.

Before I was baptized, I had never read scripture and had never received its positive influence. The first time I read the words of Jesus to "be ye therefore perfect," beings of light used those words to inspire me to try to be more like Christ. This inspiration filled me with hope and light and helped me feel closer to my Savior.

As time went on, however, my continued reference to this scripture without the Spirit leading me there became a trap to me. What started as inspiration from beings of light quickly turned a different direction. Instead of filling me with hope and light, that same scripture started to fill me with self-condemnation and despair. No matter how hard I tried, I could never be exactly like Christ.

I did not understand that no scripture is of any private interpretation, especially those that are used by beings of darkness to exercise control and dominion over us through fear, guilt, and shame. These feelings crush our faith and our ability to feel God's love. Only by releasing these arbitrary interpretations and allowing the Spirit to lead our study and understanding can we be consistently lifted in light.

One of the reasons we listen to Spirit is not to avoid judgment by God. Avoiding punishment by God is a fear based motivation. For example, consider the last time you had a prompting from God where you hesitated to follow it. What was the cause of the hesitation? And what ultimately led you to follow the prompting? Was it fear that if you didn't do it that God would not love you? Or that he would be disappointed in you? Or that you wouldn't pass your test? Or did you move forward in following the prompting because of the abundance of love and trust spontaneously flowing from your heart? Most people at a subconscious level are actually responding to promptings through fear of some sort or another.

When we release fear, guilt, and shame as motivations for following the Spirit, we continue to listen to Spirit because it reveals the true desires of our hearts. In following Spirit, we will be on that path that we need to gain the understanding and experience we came here for. We may not enjoy all of that experience in the moment. Others may even judge us for some of that experience, but we will find ourselves on the path of healing that we most need. And as we learn to trust God more deeply by having the faith and hope to follow these internal promptings, we will find that we are on the path of our highest joy.

If we make a mistake and fail to follow a prompting that we were given, then allow yourself to see the mistake in the same light that God does, with love and mercy. All experience, even what appears to be a mistake, is useful when brought into the light of God. He will consecrate all experience for our learning. It is helpful to have this faith, that even when we make a mistake God will use it to accelerate our learning and growth.

It is this belief we want to plant in our heart, that God is so loving, merciful, kind and powerful, that he can and will use even our mistakes to accelerate our growth and learning and to bless those around us. He will use all things, both our successes and our mishaps, to increase our understanding of God and the world around us. There are no mistakes before God. All things have a purpose and he has the power and the wisdom to reveal that purpose. The only question is if we are willing to let go of our guilt, shame, and other self-afflicted punishment long enough to let him show us.

We do not need to feel the punishment of our mistakes any longer than God requires, and how long does he require? Not long at all. In fact, we come to understand that all healing is through the administration of the love and mercy of God, not through punishment. Therefore, the faster we let go of the need to punish ourselves and the faster we allow God to love us, the sooner we will heal. It is God's love that changes hearts. And it is healing and the lifting of his children that is the utmost objective of God.

Let the Spirit guide you, not through compulsion, but through joy. Understand that the Spirit reveals what is in your heart, so if it gives you guidance that does not make sense to you, then ask questions about what is really in your heart and if it can change. Some specific questions in your prayers to God might be, "Can that prompting to me change or do I really need to do it? If I changed the beliefs in my heart, would the answer change? Why or why not?"

When we are children, we show faith in our parents by doing exactly as they say. As we grow older, we show faith by asking questions to help us learn. In this case, we understand that God is revealing what is in our heart through the Spirit in order for us to learn. Some lessons are easier to learn by asking questions than through the experience itself. Not all things given by Spirit were meant to be acted upon in the flesh. Some promptings are simply given to us to learn from through thought experiments.

For example, I have met a number of women who feel trapped in their marriages. Each made covenants with God to stay with her husband and feels an obligation to remain with him no matter how he treats her. Their hearts are pining for a way out of this situation while their soul wants them to learn the missing truths to heal the marriage. Consequently, the Spirit reveals this two-fold desire of their heart and ironically leads them towards healing by providing a prompting to get a divorce.

With the permission of God to move out of the marriage, they begin to think about what life would be like after the divorce. In the process of these thoughts, they discover the truths that were missing from their marriage before, ironically leading to the saving of their marriage. The prayer of their hearts changes from one requesting God's permission to leave, to giving thanks for what He has provided. Thus God's wisdom in the prompting to these women to leave their husbands was never given with the intent that it be followed, but that it be learned from through the thought experiments the women would perform in seriously considering leaving.

In my own life, I have been given promptings over the years to study hard and labor with immense effort for those in the world around me. A few years ago, I was given promptings concerning my journey of learning faith healing that would take me all over the world in a rigorous schedule that would keep me away from home for nearly six months without a break.

As I pondered this path that Spirit had given me, I began to see a different path emerge that included staying at home with my family and learning over the internet instead of doing so much travel. I realized that what I really wanted was this second path. Remembering that it is not only by faith that we receive our first prompting, but that it is also by faith that a better way is given, I asked for a better way. In this instance, my prayer was answered and I was given to follow the new desire of my heart.

Looking back, I can see that because the desires of my heart had changed in considering what the Lord had at first given me, I was given a new prompting to reflect the deeper beliefs of my heart. As we change what is in our heart, we change what is sent out and what is returned unto us. Thus, the witness of the Spirit, which is a witness of things as they really are, were and will be, is changed. That which will be is different because our hearts are now praying for something new.

This is not dissimilar from revelation changing in scriptural accounts. When Jonah delivered the message of destruction to Nineveh, what did the Spirit witness to the hearts of the people? Was it not of their assured destruction? But when they changed what was in their hearts, how did that affect the witness of the Spirit to them? Did they not then receive the peaceful assurance of a new future that was not previously described in scripture?

We cannot change the deepest thoughts, feelings, and desires of our hearts without also changing the witness of the Spirit to us. Every time we change these deep thoughts, we alter the god-thread of what will be. Therefore, the Spirit's witness to us changes.

In extreme cases, promptings come that seem to resemble Abraham's sacrifice on the mount with his son Isaac. One colleague of mine felt prompted to consider suicide. She had been shown how much growth the people in her life would have if she just took her own life. She was told, "You can see how much they would grow if you were no longer present, so if you love them, why not take your life?"

This friend called me terribly worried that she was listening to the wrong voice. I knew this friend well enough to know something about the source of her promptings. I helped her recognize the fear in her worry and then encouraged her to perform the thought experiment in order to face the fear. I told her that our Heavenly Parents love us immensely and there is a purpose in all they prompt us to do. I suggested in this case, the prompting was not to follow physically but to learn from in her mind.

When she carried the thought experiment out, she discovered that the prompting was revealing a slightly incorrect perception of charity within her. Her definition of charity was based on the idea that we sacrifice self in order to lift others; the happiness of others is more important than our own. She saw the error and recognized that true charity is love for all parties, including self, not love for those being served and hatred for self. Therefore, to sacrifice her own life for others in this way was not charity despite the growth others might receive, because it did not include God's love for her.

What is interesting is that if she had not been given this extreme prompting to consider, she never would have seen the subtle effect of a lifetime of living with a definition of Christ's love that was not quite on the mark. She had been giving and giving for others in a way that was tainted with a subtle form of self-deprecation. While as a younger Christian this was acceptable for her, the time had come for her to grow in her faith and her ability to give. It was only in this extreme prompting that she was able to find truth in such a profound way.

This was also true for Abraham as he faced the subconscious wounds placed by his own father when Abraham had been offered up as a sacrifice to false gods. Only by following such an extreme, personal prompting to then take his own son, Isaac, to the mountain was he able to truly confront the fears placed in his subconscious by his own father and find the deep and full healing at a personal level that he needed. This personal journey of faith also gave him a powerful witness of the Messiah to come. Even in the case of Abraham, this prompting was only carried so far in the flesh, but he went the full distance in his heart and in his thoughts. What makes the thought experiment powerful is the willingness to do as Abraham, actually taking the steps in our hearts that are necessary to fulfill the will of God.

This is something important to observe for those who have an increasing connection with God and start to receive Abrahamic trials of faith. Many of these trials of faith can be learned from in a far easier fashion through thought rather than in flesh. Use the thought experiment to learn from any prompting you receive. As you carry it out with real intent, you will learn from it almost the same as if you did it in the flesh. Then check back in and see if the learning and changes in belief structure in your heart result in a different instruction from God on how to proceed.

When in doubt if a prompting should be carried out in the flesh or in thought alone, ask. There are no stupid questions before God. The only stupid questions are the ones that are not asked. We are taught that God gives liberally to all those who ask of him and that he upbraids not, or rather, he never says, "That is a stupid or inappropriate question!"

In our asking God, it would do us well to let go of any residual low vibration beliefs about God. He is not a low vibration being. He is not offended by our questions. He is in a state of love, joy, and full comprehension. Let him be your best friend, your greatest resource. He is a better resource than Google. He is more loving and even faster to respond. His answers will be exactly what you need in the moment.

Remember though, that we are taught in pieces. He will give you what you need to understand today for the experience you most need, then give you the remaining pieces tomorrow to make sense of that experience. It is not that God changes his mind or that his words are not eternal, it is simply the nature of the experience we are here to have. The end is not given from the beginning and the instructions and understanding of today will not be what we are given tomorrow. There is always more to learn, more to understand, so let go of the need to understand the end from the beginning or of the need to blame God when he does not provide you the end from the beginning, and start to exercise faith. Faith is not to have a knowledge of all things in the present moment but is to trust in the goodness and wisdom of God, no matter where the journey leads us.

For your consideration:

- Close your eyes and reflect, what is your true motivation in following Spirit? Are there any promptings you follow where this is not the case? Imagine and especially feel what life would be like if you were to follow promptings out of a more pure motive, out of an abundance of love and trust for God. What do you notice?
- What sources do you listen to without checking in with Spirit? Are there any instructions you have received from these sources that might be different if you did check in with Spirit? What would your life be like if you did take the Spirit to be your guide in all things?
- Reflect on your past promptings. Are there any you could have learned from with a thought exercise without needing to act on it in the flesh? Would this have been better or worse? Why?
- Reflect on your current promptings and have a conversation with God. Are there any of your current promptings that might change if a belief in your heart changed? Are any of these promptings meant to be followed in thought exercises instead of carried out in real life?
- Take one of your current promptings, close your eyes and envision what happens as you follow it. What emotions arise? What do you learn about yourself? Does this give you new ideas for how to follow the prompting? Use what you learned to ask God more details about your prompting.

CHAPTER

14

Faith in Grace

The appearance of new understanding can have multiple effects. One of those is that we feel empowered, as though our hope has been added to greatly. We see the chance to use the power of spiritual creation to fix our lives, to solve the hurts. Understanding how to modify the subconscious can lead to a desire to clear out all the hurt and be pure before God.

The problem with this is that the same old patterns are playing out in a new game. Now instead of trying to control the physical world with physical action, we simply move to a new field: the field of the heart and mind. The same players now want to play the new game, to control the outcome, to use fear, grief, guilt, and shame as motivation to change our internal and external world.

Instead of relieving our burden, our burden can actually feel heavier. Now we not only feel responsible for our physical actions but also our mental and emotional ones, even those that lay beneath our conscious awareness. If the previous burden was impossible to carry, this newer burden is even more so.

In all of our journey, we should remember the words of Christ, that his burden is easy, his yoke is light. He bid all the weary of heart and mind to come unto him, to take his burden upon him.

As we step into this new world of understanding, it is helpful to know that grace is still the answer. Even after all of our efforts, all of our learning, all of our doing, it is still by grace that we are saved. In fact, even the progress we appear to make with our effort is still powered by grace. The learning and progress we make are not because of our church attendance, our diligence in service, or any other thing, but despite it, coming from the pure fountain of God's good will and love. When the subconscious motive of "earning" God's love is released along with the attendant fear, guilt, and shame, our actions are done out of love and joy from a pure heart. We need no more external motive to do them because we do them automatically as part of what we are. The more we understand this, the lighter our burden will be, the less frustrated we will be when our progress is not as fast or in the way that we wanted.

Grace really is the key component of letting go. Whether a person recognizes Jesus as the author of grace or not, it is through grace that they receive all knowledge and understanding of God, all healing, all growth.

It is through grace that God causes his sun to shine upon all peoples of all religious understandings and dispositions. The sun is a symbol of truth, of light and knowledge, of understanding of God, of joy, of hope and of peace. It is a symbol of truth present in Christ. God is not offended by name calling, especially not those names given to him with sincere honor and respect by members of all faiths. He answers the prayers of all who have faith, no matter what name they approach him through. And it is through these answered prayers that he leads all of his children into an increased understanding and access to truth. Thus, he freely, willingly and lovingly pours out his light upon all, even as much as they are willing to receive.

Whether or not a person understands the fullness of the stature, purpose, and meaning of Christ, they have access to grace. After all, how many of us now upon the earth truly understand Christ? If it were a prerequisite to understand him before receiving any of his light, then perhaps none of us would qualify to make the journey.

Whether we understand the source of the electricity that powers our home or not, we still have access to it. We still use it. It still powers and enriches our lives. Understanding it can help us implement it in more useful ways, especially if we are those engineers whose jobs include distributing the light to others. But for the world at large, they can receive the majority of the benefit without ever understanding the source.

This is what is meant by God's sun rising upon the righteous and the wicked. His light, his love, and his mercy are provided universally, whether or not we understand it. The blessings of God, the outpourings of knowledge could not be held back even if we tried to stop it.

None of the religious moorings or understandings that have ever existed in the history of the earth have ever been able to stop God from pouring out further light and knowledge upon his people. In every generation, there have been those who have tried to use the legitimate teachings of God to prevent further light and knowledge from being granted. The Pharisees and the Sadducees formed their offense against Christ and his apostles with the legitimate law given by God, but they failed to stop the outpouring of light and so will every individual who uses religious principles to restrict light.

We love God. We love his light. We seek after all things that are good, noble, virtuous or pure. Wherever there is any light of God, we claim the right to lay hold on these things. And we understand that his light is in all things and through all things. It simply takes more discerning eyes, more patient eyes, to see the light where it is at.

When we can see the light in all things, we will have greater joy in our journey. There will be less fight against those things that be. Even to the extent that there is darkness, we see the light, or rather the purpose in it. We feel God's love and appreciation for all things, because all things work together for our good because God is that great.

We understand that no matter what happens, we are on a journey that leads back to Him. We are on a journey of which he is the author and finisher of our faith. By letting go, we find our minds quickened, our hearts elevated and our journey enhanced.

Like a lazy river ride, there is little we can do to accelerate or slow the journey that has been placed before us. Rather, with faith in the Creator of all things, we let go and enjoy the journey. It is my belief that by enjoying the journey, by having this degree of faith in God, we open ourselves to the greatest degree of growth possible for us in this life.

The power behind the lazy river ride is not one of our own action or force of will. It is of grace. Although we may appear to kick or paddle forward or backward, the current which leads us through all things is not our own. The divine plan that was formed before this world moves us.

While we have agency within that plan, almost all choices will lead us to the same conclusion. In the end, we will know who we are and the desires of our own hearts. There will be no mistakes. God is not an administrator of a timed, state standard exam for which we have not been prepared. He is the merciful custodian of the love that is in all things and through all things, the love of which he is a fullness.

He has all knowledge and all understanding. While we are here to learn, this is not a test. We can never fail to earn God's love. It is given freely because he is love. All we can do is to choose to defer it. We can run away into the utmost ends of the universe, commit the most heinous acts to try to make him stop loving us, but like a persistent and patient parent, we can never escape his love.

The burning pains of those who are in a state of hell are not from the lack of God's love, but rather from the fact that no matter how unworthy those who are in that state feel, they cannot escape his love. They cannot find any place in existence that was not created by God, that is not full of his light and the ever-present reminder of his unfailing love. It is the unworthiness burned into their own minds, their own self-judgment, that causes the pain and the anguish. It is self-rejection of all that God wants to pour out upon us that keeps us in darkness, in this life, and in the world to come.

When we acknowledge that every gift comes through grace, that we are the gatekeepers to how much we receive and when we receive it, then we can begin to let go more fully. We can begin to allow God to pour more out upon us. We can cease to deny his love and mercy and allow it to enter into us, to heal us, to change our hearts.

Heaven is not a place so much as it is a state of being. This is why heaven cannot be found when we have failed to allow God's love to change our hearts. It is not a condemnation, but a simple fact. Our hearts draw to us the joys and the pains we experience. Unless we allow God to place heaven in our heart, we can never comprehend or be in a state of heaven. Again, it is by grace that we are saved. We simply decide if and when to let go and the degree to which we will allow change on any given day.

This change is not dictated by the choice of the conscious mind so much as by the choice of the heart. Since we have so little control over our own hearts at present, then we must return to faith. We must hope that God is wonderful, merciful and kind. We must place our lives in his hands and yield most fully and completely. Although all the effort and learning are wonderful, in the end, it is by grace that we are saved, even after all we can do.

So why labor or study? Because it is our joy to do so. Our motivation changes from one of necessity to one of love and joy. When all other motivations cease to exist, when grace has been accepted, when we have let go of our lives and yielded unto God all our subconscious motivations, then love and joy are what is left. Thus, we are engaged in a labor of love where what it is that we are to be is not yet apparent. We only know that when he shall appear, we shall be like him, for we shall see him as he is. And everyone who has this hope in him, purifies themselves, even as he is pure.

For your consideration:

- Close your eyes and reflect. Does the yoke you are carrying feel light or does it feel heavy? If it is burdensome at all, what would it feel like to take Christ's yoke of grace more fully upon you? If Christ's name has been misused to burden you in the past, what would it feel like just to receive through grace? What would be the best thing about that?
- What areas of your life are you trying to change the flow of the lazy river in? Are you resisting the flow or trying to move faster than it? Is it the same in each area of your life? Work? Home? Family? Spiritual life? Close your eyes and relax. What are the real reasons you are afraid to let go and move at the rate God is moving you?

CHAPTER

15

The Flow That Puts It All Together

When we look at life, it should be joyful. We are here for joy, which sometimes seems ironic because joy is often the last emotion that we feel. But we are not here to feel joy without understanding. We had joy freely given to us before this life. Here, we inherit a state of opposition and adversity and have a chance to improve our real-estate, to truly comprehend the substance of joy by reverse engineering it out of a quasi-hell.

When we see life, we see all sorts of individuals teaching different paths to joy. None of what is taught is final or complete. Whether purely secular or religious in nature, each is riddled with subconscious beliefs and views on what will bring us greater contentment. Because of the subconscious impurities, each has an experience which leads them somewhere other than where they thought.

For example, many people today have embraced the idea that it is important to take "me time." The principle behind this is that it is easier to give from a full cup than an empty cup, so taking the necessary time to love and fill ourselves with light is consistent with God's love for us. Although this is a true principle that builds on self-love, subconscious impurities often transform this attempt at self-love into self-medication, or in other words, the use of entertainment and other pleasures to avoid dealing with the hurt in our soul. Thus our subconscious impurities corrupt a true principle and instead of filling our cup, can lead to a drain on resources including time and money. In addition, it can potentially lead to developing addictive behavior with our chosen entertainment or activity and weakening the connection with friends and loved ones from the drain on our time and emotions spent engaging in the activity. Thus, the healing concept of "me time" is morphed by our subconscious impurities into an excuse to disconnect rather than an opportunity to reconnect.

In this world, none of us, or at least none of the human portions of us, seem to know where to find that true joy. Every true principle is tainted with the limitations of our mortal understanding. Even our brightest ideas are just the brightness of the stars compared to that of the moon or the sun. Only when we release to that part of us that is whole and complete are we shown the way. It is the part of us that is already whole that is able to reconstruct heaven upon earth. It is the part of us that is in perfect connection with God that knows how to make what we seek upon this earth. It is in the letting go, not in the fight, that we find heaven.

To the degree that we discover heaven within us, we shall see it start to materialize without us. That is, it will both materialize in the world around us and without our having to lift a hand to make it so. This is faith by power, the faith to let go and let God.

Heaven does not exist because of our own merit or might or intelligence. It is not through force that heaven is created. It is just the opposite. Heaven is a product of the cessation of force, what remains when all force is released.

When we look into our souls we often times do not know or understand how to let go in this way or to continue upon the path. The answer is simpler perhaps than we realize. In this book, we have discussed working with beliefs and emotions. We have discussed heart-centered awareness and other concepts, touching upon much of the best wisdom available at this time. However, at the end of the day, almost all of this can be simplified into a single concept or idea: Flow.

Flow is the river. It is the wind in the sky. It is the waves and tides of the ocean. It is the cycle of life and death. It is movement. It is allowance. It is the opposite of the dam in the river, the opposite of the wall blocking the wind. It is the opposite of every form or resistance. Spirit is flow. Life is flow.

In the human body, whenever the fluidity of joints is disrupted, there is disease, arthritis, pain. Whenever the fluidity of the immune system is disrupted, there is sickness and death. Wherever the blood flow is disrupted, there is malnutrition, hypoxia, and cell apoptosis. Without the flow of the physical body, there is physical death. Without the flow of thought, emotion and spirit, there is also death of a different sort.

We use beliefs to access emotions. We use emotion to access flow. When we first learn to work with the subconscious, we use beliefs in the form of words as a handle to access places within us that are no longer flowing. The words form an interface with the logical mind, a way for the logical mind to connect with emotion, emotion forming the vehicle to access flow.

While beliefs are a wonderful access point, they can become cumbersome and slow if we allow our rigidity with needing to access words to limit us. Like a dam in our own progression through consciousness work, the need to use words can block our flow. While the use of words can help get the flow moving, at some point, we need to move beyond them.

The words in belief work can help us to start recognizing the presence and identity of emotion. It gives the logical mind a means to understand what these emotions are and where they come from. It allows the left brain to engage with the purpose behind the emotional experience.

As the brain starts to pattern what the emotions are, where they come from and how to work with them in meaningful ways, the training wheels of belief work can start to come off. This does not mean that we cease to value belief work or never use it again. Rather, more powerful tools become available and we return to belief work only as we are directed to through our inner guidance and personal joy.

Working with emotion becomes a much more direct way of engaging flow. We can feel the emotions and our resistance to either feeling them or letting them go. Thus the emotions get us one step closer to working with pure flow. But they of themselves are still not the thing itself. They are just a more powerful handle on where there is resistance and where there is flow.

By working with emotion without the need to label them with beliefs and logic, there is a more powerful system for shifting rigidity within us. One emotion can cover many, many beliefs in a single swath. It is a connection to many life events where similar feelings were had. It is a more direct access point to rigidity within our subconscious. Ultimately, we want to feel where we are stuck and where we are flowing. We want to be able to let go of the rigidity, with or without identifying the beliefs and emotions behind it.

So what exactly is this rigidity? For a breadwinner, imagine yourself in a situation where you lose your job. Imagine taking a risk to go out and start that business you always wanted to. Imagine spending money beyond your normal limits. For a mother, imagine what would happen if you did not teach your children a secular education to prepare them for their future. Imagine what would happen if you failed to instill religious or spiritual truth in them. Whatever your trigger is, imagine it and notice what shows up.

As you do this thought exercise, what emotions arise? Sometimes we are unable to recognize the rigidity at first, but we can see the emotion of fear or discomfort, or even the thoughts of the logical mind that immediately arise to tell us how irrational that would be. For the mind that cannot yet recognize rigidity, notice the emotion. For the soul that cannot yet connect with emotion, notice thought. Each of these is a function of rigidity. Like a wave rebounding off a wall, they are evidence of the blockage to flow.

But if the actions we are considering in our thought exercise are emotionally unstable or irrational or illogical in any way, then why would we ever consider doing them? The problem lies not with the doing, but rather with the rigidity. Every area of rigidity is an area where faith and spirit are not flowing. There is a resistance to belief within us. The subconscious roots of this resistance are often fear, hurt or other pain. There is a fear to even try lest we meet failure and find hurt. Thus, our fear shuts down our faith. Wherever there is fear, faith is not. If we are to develop faith as a principle of power, the type of faith to rend the veil, then we must learn to release all of our fears and our jealousies.

Every time we notice these thoughts or emotions arising, we can immediately become aware that the problem is not in the world around us, it is not with our own actions even, but rather with the obstruction to the flow of faith and spirit. When we feel this rigidity, one of the most powerful ways of shifting it is to simply let go with the intention of allowing God and angels to do the rest, to move whatever needs to be moved in your physical, mental, emotional or spiritual world.

As discussed previously, dropping into a heart-centered awareness where there is no thought, emotion or doer to be found is one of the easiest ways to let go. Coupled with this intent is the willingness to allow God to take over, to submit and yield the heart unto God so that it may be more fully purified.

When our hearts are purified, even without ever having to consciously understand the blocks that were there, we will notice no more obstruction to flow. Where there was once rigidity and emotional or mental pain or resistance, now there is peace. There are a simple acceptance and allowance. Where before there was doubt or fear, now there is trust and faith in God.

While we can identify the one area in our life that is most troubling to us and release the rigidity in it, we do not have to stop there. We can release the rigidity to faith in all things. We can have faith as a grain of mustard seed in all areas of our lives, with the power to produce miracles. This is an ongoing process and evolution that changes not only us but the world around us.

Because the light within us is in all things and through all things, our consciousness is not an island. All that we think and all that we release has an impact on the world around us. As we rise, so does the world. Our purity of heart, of thinking, of being, is what allows the light of the world to increase to the point that Jesus can return.

Every thought we release not only opens us to greater flow but sends ripple effects throughout the entire world to elevate the whole. We open the world as a whole to greater faith, light, and possibilities. As the world rises, there will be some who choose to exit, who do not wish to be a part of the joy that is coming. Their learning is not done with the fallen world, so they will exit to go to a place where they can continue their learning for the time being. However, their choice does not have to limit our faith or our progression. It is our joy to rise and to lift the world with us.

Thus, it is not only our rigidity that evaporates, but we loosen the rigidity of consciousness of the earth itself. We provide room for the collective faith to ascend to the heavens and call down the light of heaven upon us.

The changes possible in our world go far beyond the conveniences in our own lives. Where do you feel rigidity with what is possible in the progression of your own religion? In the political or economic environment? In the peaceful transition of the world into a state of light? In the possibility for heaven to literally exist upon earth, to be present during that dispensation? Where is your faith blocked? Do you want to stay blocked, or are you willing to allow God to purify your heart to allow you to have faith and trust in all things, not just the few that are on the surface of your mind?

This trust and faith in God take on the form of submission of the infant to its parents. There is a willingness to allow God to move us into all experience. There is a trust that no matter what experience arises, it is perfectly suited to us. We are no longer victims where life is constantly happening *to* us, but life becomes a gift in every regard where all things are continuously happening *for* us. This is flow. This is trust. This is faith. This is the state of grace where we most want to be, where all things are consecrated for our growth and our benefit.

For your consideration:

- What do you notice that is stuck? Where is emotion rigidly holding something in place? What feels like it can never change? What stuck places are you ignoring by justifying that these things *should* never change?
- Try connecting with something in your life that feels stuck. Feel into the emotion, then connect that emotion to the light in Christ with your intention (visualization can sometimes help) and drop into

your heart to let go. Keep dropping into your heart for several moments, giving permission for him to open the flow to faith and change anything that needs to change. What do you notice? What is different?

CHAPTER

16

The Revelation of Jesus Christ

As I have pondered mirrors in the world around us and how all things reflect some part inside of us, I have noticed that the biggest mirrors of all are often our spouses and those of our own family. With the many things our spouses do that bring up hurt, grief or frustration, they unknowingly point to the areas within us that most need our healing love and attention.

In my own marriage, there was a time when I would push away from my wife's pain and frustration. In resonance with a typical male consciousness, I believed that if I took time to listen to her, I would feel her emotion and it would make me less productive and capable as a provider. I would feel less productive as a provider because the emotional pain I felt from feeling responsible for her happiness and failing to provide that happiness would shut down my ability to just grit my teeth and get my job done at work. Since my role as a provider was where most of my value was, I feared her emotion. I feared her pain, and I shunned it at all costs.

As I turned inward and learned about the mirrors in our lives, I began to see that her pain was a reflection of my own hurt. That is not to say that her fears and hurts were my own, but that my fear of her hurt and her pain was really a reflection of the fear of my own emotion and my fear of failing as a provider, as a husband and a father. Because I was afraid of my own emotion, I could not handle hers. Her continuous emotional state was, in fact, a mirror to show me my own fear and the healing that needed to take place within me. All things that arise show us where we need more love and tenderness, but our spouses hold a special role in that regard.

As this knowledge became more clear, I saw that to embrace her in her hurt was not a weakness, but a strength. I did not endanger my own emotional health or stability by being around her in her hurt. Rather, with each hug I gave her, with each "I love you," I was not only embracing her but the hurt places inside of me as well. The more fully I loved her, even and especially in her emotional state, the more fully I loved and embraced the parts of me that felt abandoned or afraid.

When we fully understand the concept of mirrors, we understand that they have been given to us for our own healing. Not necessarily so that we will turn inward, but so that through our outward focus and tenderness to all who come into our space, we can find love and healing for those places within us that we could not formerly see.

The more diligently we love others, embracing those places in them that hurt or frustrate us, the more diligently we invite God's light and healing into our own space. By more fully loving them in their weakness, we can more easily release the self-condemnation from our own weakness and have more tenderness and mercy on ourselves. Since we are all connected through the light that is in all things and through all things, loving them is loving a neglected piece of ourselves. When we can see the outer as a reflection of the inner, then healing is possible through embracing others more deeply and fully.

In terms of bride and bridegroom analogies, scripture teaches us that Jesus is the ultimate bridegroom and we are his bride. If all things are mirrors and our spouses are our greatest mirrors, what is it that Jesus reveals in us? What was it that he came to show or teach us? There is a reflection of truth about each of us in his every action, in the full view of his life.

When Jesus looked at someone, he saw them as they were. There was no ego left in him to obscure the reflection of what is in us. This is why to look in the eyes of Christ is a moving event. It is not just that we have been granted access to his presence, it is that we receive of a revelation of who and what we are. We see ourselves in his eyes. It is this truth which is painful for the wicked to see. It is this truth which will set us free if we will allow ourselves to receive it.

The truth is not painful to the wicked because he sees wickedness or casts blame or disappointment. Rather the truth is painful because of the light he sees within us. What he sees is the ultimate reversal of our beliefs about ourselves. He sees underneath all the dirt and the muck that we believe is our life; he sees the light within. He sees the innocence of the newborn within us because the light of God within us can never be dirtied. It can never be darkened; it can only be covered through disbelief.

But he sees it. He sees us as we truly are and this is his revelation to those who can bear the intensity of it.

To the woman taken in adultery, Jesus said, "Neither do I condemn thee." (John 8:11) To the soldiers who crucified him, he said, "Father, forgive them; for they know not what they do." (Luke 23:34) He loved us more than his own life and taught us that this was truth. He did not bring himself to love us because it was the "right" thing to do. He did not do it out of fear of punishment. He did not do it to find a reward or to escape the pain of his life. He did it because he saw something. He saw truth. The truth was inside of him and he lived that truth.

When we see Jesus for who he is, we see that the revelation he came to give was of our own divine nature. It is witnessed in every action he took. His entire life bore witness of the worth of the nature and worth of the innocence within us. He embodied the light in its fullness not to show us our limitations, but to reveal to us our potential.

In this life, there are many potential mirrors. There are many women I could have married and made a life with. But the angel who was appointed to lead me back to my Father in Heaven, the angel who was appointed to be my mirror and lovingly help me see the areas that most need healing was the woman I chose to marry. This is a role that is exclusively hers in this life. It was the role that she and I and Father determined before his life. I love her for it. I appreciate her for it, and I am not less for seeing or acknowledging that role. In fact, my light is increased as I lift her in the way that lifts me.

It is part of being human to have compassion, to have compassion on our own humanness and frailty. We know what we want to be. We want to be perfect servants. But we are not. We fall short repeatedly, never understanding that this is, in fact, God's perfection. It is not humanity's perfection that we are after, but after the perfect experience we came here to have. It is perfectly acceptable to have compassion on our weakness when we fail to receive our spouses as fully as we would like. We can have compassion on the hurt places within us that are reflected in our spouses when we fail to live up to our true potential.

There were many amazing teachers in this life who might have been selected to play the role that Jesus did. But he was the one anointed before this life by Father and sustained by the rest of us to be that mirror. He was the one appointed to bring the revelation from on high of who we really are. And that revelation did not stop with divinity but continued by revealing the power of God over death. Although there have been many teachers on this earth who have become a fullness of light, like Enoch and his entire city who were taken up unto God, Christ was the one appointed to reveal our divinity not just through death, but through resurrection.

What is it that he reflects in us? What is it that he teaches us? Does his reflection limit us in any way? Was he not the one who taught us that we would not be limited because he went to his Father, that greater things we would yet do? Do we understand that his life and sacrifice were not just for us to talk about on Sundays, but so that we could comprehend our own nature? Do we see the gift of faith as a principle of power he gave us in his revelation of our identities and potential in this life?

As I studied so many other ideas and systems of faith, I feared that I would lose my faith. Each time I saw people who were good, compassionate and loving heal another person through faith, I worried. Where was there room for my faith in Christ when so many of the people who had the signs spoken of in scripture were non-Christian? Where were the Christian saints? Had faith ceased from the earth?

As I saw that the root of most Christian faith is based on fear, guilt, and shame, my faith took another blow. Was there any good thing in the Christian religions, or was it all the very force and control we came here to overcome? What did this mean about Christ, the father of Christian religion? My faith took one hit after another, yet I still felt the voice of God telling me to press on, to complete my scientific observation. I felt that somehow all of this tied to an even deeper understanding and faith in Christ.

I believe that it is God's desire that we not only have a superficial understanding of him or of the role of Christ in this world but that we come to a knowledge of the fullness of his stature. "And this is life eternal, that they might know thee the only true God, and Jesus Christ, whom thou hast sent." (John 17:3)

The light within God must be purified from our subconscious limitations. That which is truth must be separated from that which is superstition. Johannes Kepler once feared the truth of what he discovered behind his telescope. At that time, the belief that the heavens were perfect was connected to the perfection of geometry. Since God dwelt in the heavens, the orbits of the planets and the stars must be perfect. There was no more perfect geometry than the circle, but this was not what Kepler observed in the planetary orbits. What he observed was heresy according to the beliefs of his day, but he could not deny what he saw.

As a true Christian, Kepler did all in his power to disprove what he had seen. He could not be the one who brought forth evidence that the faith of all Christianity at that time was incorrect. He went into hiding for a period of years where he studied furiously. Who knows what trials his soul went through at that time. While for us, this scientific observation might seem trivial, for his subconscious cultural programming, it was a matter of God's existence and perfection.

In time, he discovered truth. His sustained faith that God would reveal all paid off. He discovered that the planets did have a perfect, mathematical orbit. The math behind the elliptical orbit of the planets was far more beautiful and perfect than anything contained within the circle. His faith was not only sustained but led to even greater truths.

Like those who lived in the days of Kepler, too often what we see around us that seems to challenge our faith is dismissed. Our faith is too weak to accept the invitation from God to grow. We do not see it as God's own hand inviting us to look deeper, to find a faith, a comprehension and a joy that we could never have had otherwise.

As we see the world in a new light, it can challenge our religious beliefs; it can cause us to question the nature of existence itself. This process of reformation is, in fact, a really deep process of rebirth. It is the process of us coming to see the very innocence within us that Christ has always seen, that he came to reflect within us.

This process of rebirth is not always comfortable. It is not always quick and easy. It can cost us everything we believed true about life. But in the end, the process of rebirth is just another invitation to yield unto God in even deeper ways than we ever have before. It is in this process of complete submission, even as a newborn to its parents, that we are purified before God. It is in that day that we shall see ourselves as he sees us.

It is my personal witness that not only does the light exist within us that connects us to all things, but Jesus Christ is a fullness of that light. While there have been others and will be others who receive a fullness, yet Jesus was the one appointed to reveal that light on this earth. He was the one appointed to reveal a fullness of God's love and of salvation, not just from an illusory and self-created hell, but from the lesser ideas of heaven that occlude our progression.

Because we are divine, whatever idea we plant in our hearts comes into being. The endless heavens described in the philosophies of humankind are all real precisely because we plant these ideas in our hearts. It has been my privilege to see some of these heavens and they are beautiful beyond compare.

But because we create these heavens by the ideas we plant in our hearts, they are limited by what we can comprehend. They are bounded by the subconscious limitations of our understanding. Therefore, these heavens conceived by men populate the glories described by Paul that are like the brightness of the stars or the moon. But to create a heaven which shines brighter than the sun, we must plant a purer seed than can be bounded by human understanding. The fruit cannot be greater than the seed we plant in our hearts.

Salvation with a capital "S," or exaltation, is the planting of a seed beyond all others. When properly understood, it is the planting of a joy beyond even the comprehension of the gods. It is the original creation that brought us as children of the divine to this earth. Connecting with this frequency is to connect with the reason we came here to begin with. It is to wake up not only to our ability to create but also to what it was we came here to create: a joy beyond all imagination or possibility to comprehend. It is a joy which eye has not seen, nor ear heard, nor entered into the heart of man.

A couple of years ago, I had a multi-hour experience similar to a near-death experience in which I was taken up into the heavens. The intensity of the love and joy was overwhelming causing me to feel that my body would have died if I had been in my body. At the end of my time there, I was given a tour, but not of the buildings or the people. Rather, I was given a tour of the physics behind the creation and structure of the heavens. I saw that the light that is in all things and through all things is the light of which God is a fullness. I saw that this light is within us as well and that whatever we put in our hearts is brought back to us.

Then I was shown that the seemingly infinite joy I was then experiencing in the presence of God was not bounded or limited. Simply by planting the belief that there was even greater joy, even greater love, the light of God in all things would respond to that prayer of my heart and bring it back to me even as it was in my heart. I did not have to know how, I only needed to know that it would be brought back. My faith made it so. Faith was literally the key to the structure of the ever-expanding nature of the heavens.

Have you never considered that the highest heaven may not be a static state? Rather than the static view of either the East or the West, of the Christian view of people playing harps for eternity or the Buddhist view of dissolving back into the light for eternity, what if the highest heaven consists of continuous and everlasting change? What if the state God exists within is, in fact, a state of ever-increasing glory?

Accordingly, Salvation with a capital "S" is the frequency of light that Jesus revealed of an ever-expanding progression into an unending and eternal heaven. It is the awakening from the limiting perceptions of the truths of yesterday into a more glorious understanding of the future. Even as Jesus's suffering was so great that even he, God, trembled and bled from every pore, now his joy is so great that even he, God, is continually surprised at the intensity of it. It is as though not only Christ but also our Father in Heaven, is a child on Christmas morning, continually and joyfully surprised by the dawning of a new day and the gifts it will hold.

Salvation is a continuous process of awakening from the joys and perceptions of the heaven we had yesterday into the surprising and delicious expanse of a new and more glorious heaven of today where faith is the medium of our eternal progression. It is the continual rebirth of understanding, constant growth. There is no end. There is no limit.

Loving him more fully is not a weakness. By embracing the Mirror of Salvation more fully, we embrace those parts in us that he reflects; we embrace our access to the concept and power of Salvation within us. By loving and reverencing him, we reverence our own light and divinity and the God who gave us that light and divinity. By loving Christ, we bring more healing power into ourselves. By planting this real seed of incomprehensible joy in our hearts, we bring back to us the ultimate manifestation which brought us here to begin with. And thus, it is by his stripes that we are healed.

"Beloved, now are we the sons of God, and it doth not yet appear what we shall be: but we know that, when he shall appear, we shall be like him; for we shall see him as he is. And every man that hath this hope in him purifieth himself, even as he is pure." (I John 3:2-3)

For your consideration:

- As we move into the millennial time, there will be no more fear, guilt or shame. There will be no more death or hell to be saved from. What is the role of Christ and salvation in that world? What about in the world beyond the millennial time? If your faith in Christ is based on any degree of fear, guilt or shame, is that a stable foundation for the future? What would be a more stable foundation to build with him?
- Why do many spiritual non-Christians refuse to even consider the truths of Christ? How might that change if our belief in him was based on pure love free from any taint of fear, guilt, and shame? How might our behavior around others not of our belief system change?

- What does Christ mirror or reveal in you that you love most about yourself? How does embracing him more fully help you to embrace that part of yourself?
- Have a conversation with God. Talk to him openly about your fears and your doubts. Be honest with Him. Talk to Him about what you want to know more of, where you want to grow. Having the faith to express the prayer of your heart is one of the best ways to see it answered.
- Do you believe that you can receive a personal witness of Jesus Christ? What does seeing God in the external environment reflect in your internal state of being? How could this increase your joy? What is blocking your faith to have this experience?

If you enjoyed the book, please consider leaving a review or sharing your thoughts in a blog post so others can share in your joy.

For additional information on the book or for updates on future books and classes by Brent or Jennifer Satterfield, please visit:

www.faithtoproducemiracles.com

CPSIA information can be obtained
at www.ICGtesting.com
Printed in the USA
BVHW071454250319
543610BV00002B/181/P

9 781504 398527